THE CHANCE TO GROW

The Chance to Grow

✦✦✦✦✦✦✦✦✦✦✦✦✦✦✦✦✦✦✦✦✦✦✦✦✦✦✦✦✦✦✦✦✦✦✦✦✦✦✦

Katherine Froman

EVEREST HOUSE
Publishers
New York

LIBRARY OF CONGRESS CATALOGING IN PUBLICATION DATA:

FROMAN, KATHERINE.
THE CHANCE TO GROW.

INCLUDES BIBLIOGRAPHIES.
1. HANDICAPPED CHILDREN—CARE AND TREATMENT—
UNITED STATES. I. TITLE.
HV888.5F76   1983   362.4'088054   82-25275
ISBN 0-89696-192-3

PUBLISHED BY EVEREST HOUSE,
79 MADISON AVENUE, NEW YORK, N.Y. 10016
PUBLISHED SIMULTANEOUSLY IN CANADA BY
MCCLELLAND AND STEWART LIMITED, TORONTO
MANUFACTURED IN THE UNITED STATES OF AMERICA
DESIGNED BY JUDITH LERNER
FIRST EDITION
FG483

TO MY MOTHER AND MY CHILDREN
who are teaching me about mothering

TO MY HUSBAND
who gives me love and friendship

TO ALL MY BABIES AND THEIR FAMILIES
who are showing me
what caring and commitment can do

CONTENTS

FOREWORD

THIS BOOK is about one of the most hopeful and least publicized developments in modern medicine—the change during the last decade toward humane and effective treatment of handicapped infants and young children.

It reports the development, as I have observed it in my own work, in physical therapy with several such children and their sometimes heroic families. At certain points the intensity of their lives approached the outer reaches of human experience.

The events described in the book are real. To protect the privacy of the people involved I have changed not only their names but also all the recognizable details of their stories. Any resemblance to actual individuals is a coincidence.

Because I took up my profession at the time when the new way of treating these children was getting established, the book also tells my own story of, to parody the old cliché, girl meets career, girl loses career, girl gets career.

During my work with handicapped babies and young children, I developed a personal solution for the problem of "burnout," the emotional exhaustion that eventually cripples many who work in the helping professions. I have been able to avoid it by working no more than 20–25 hours a week and seeing regularly only 10 or 12 children. It is a solution that can enhance both the self-respect and the value to the community of many women who, like me, take a few years to raise families and then want to go back to work.

But what I have tried to do most of all in writing this book is to help others share and understand the varying ways of

9

life of some children whose lives are different from those of most people, the difference beginning at their birth. The more the general public knows about these children, the less the children will suffer rejection and revulsion. I have learned a great deal from them and hope that I can pass on some of it to you.

KATHERINE FROMAN
San Luis Obispo, Calif.
January, 1983

THE CHANCE TO GROW

1
Getting Involved

About a quarter of a million handicapped infants are born in this country each year. In more barbaric times the prescribed treatment for such babies was exposure on a hillside; in other words, they were thrown away. More recently, the prescription usually was institutionalization; this was another kind of throwing away. But in the last decade the medical establishment has begun to realize how much it owes to and how much it can do for such infants. In my opinion this advance is more meaningful than a whole pharmacopeia of over-advertised wonder drugs.

I reached that opinion through some deeply moving experiences. When a child is about to be born, all concerned usually anticipate the event with hope and pleasure. When it is born with great and obvious deformities, all concerned—very much including the medical personnel—are stunned with horror. Some people never move beyond that stage. For others it becomes a stepping stone to a transfiguring kind of love—a statement which is bound to seem to some readers a form of pseudo-religious cant. In fact, I have repeatedly witnessed such transfigurations.

I am a physical therapist. Early in high school I decided that I wanted to be a nurse, but then I chanced to see a film about a therapist who worked with handicapped children. That film chose my profession for me. Volunteer work in a swim program for handicapped children confirmed the choice. Inside those distorted bodies were human beings who desperately needed to learn to cope with the cruelties life had imposed on them.

In other words, my choice of profession was emotional. The deliberately (one could even say conscientiously) cool and uninvolved specialist who concentrates all attention on solid facts provided by laboratory tests and, as far as possible, ignores the messily human patient is often quite common in many branches of medicine. Although we used to be nudged in that direction during training, physical therapists working with handicapped children simply cannot stay uninvolved. And it is deep involvement with such children that has shown again and again that a great many of these children can progress much further than expected and live much fuller lives.

Simmons College in Boston, where I studied in the late fifties when doubts about "homes for the feeble minded" and other such institutions were beginning to be voiced, is affiliated with Massachusetts General Hospital and Children's Medical Center and has one of the country's most prestigious programs in physical therapy training. I learned a great deal about how to dissect a cadaver, how to set up a program of therapeutic exercise, how to operate a diathermy machine, how to teach a crippled child to walk, and how to stand up when a person entitled to write M.D. after her or his name entered the room. I learned a little about how to cope with my patients' discomfort and pain and how to encourage or insist on the prescribed ten leg lifts and such. I learned almost nothing about how to approach my patients' fear, anger, guilt, anxiety, disbelief, denial, and other such basic problems.

"The Art and Science of Uninvolvement" was not a course listed in the catalog. It was a seldom discussed but always implicit part of every course in which we dealt with patients or were lectured on the subject of dealing with patients. On those few occasions when the subject was brought into the open, the message was emphatic. For instance:

"It is especially important to keep your professional distance in the unlikely event that emergency makes it necessary to call at the home of a patient. Under no cir-

cumstance should you accept food or drink in such a
situation, not even so much as a glass of water."

How this sort of thing came to be accepted is not clear to
me. It certainly was not accepted by old-fashioned doctors.
Their deep involvement with their patients occasionally meant
a lot of emotional pain for such practitioners, and many wore
themselves out in their round-the-clock-and-calendar efforts
to share and alleviate suffering. It is obvious that that way of
life appeals to few physicians or other health professionals
now. But those who must try to persuade themselves and
others that it is "unprofessional" to share *any* of their patients' suffering simply do not belong in this work.

Because physical therapists are not required to make decisions risking our patients' lives, it is less important for us
to keep emotional distance between them and us. Another
factor became vividly clear to me in my third year of training.
There were ten of us in my class, all women. During the first
two of our four-and-a-half years it was all book and laboratory work, mostly in the basic sciences, and not until the third
year did we begin our first specific course for physical therapists—massage. We had spent much time together during the
previous two years and had talked often about why we were
in that school and that course, and we felt intimately friendly.
But when we began, under our instructor, to give each other
massage, our intimacy deepened astonishingly. The essence of
physical therapy is just such laying of hands on the patient's
body. You have to fight really hard to stay cold and remote
when you are doing that.

Yet the pressure to fight that hard fight was powerful during my years of training. We were assured over and over
again that cool objectivity was in the best interest of our patients. I do not know how well or how long I would have
resisted such neatly rationalized pressure if I had stayed in
the professional groove and, after graduation, had gone to
work with adult patients in a hospital. But my years off, to-

gether with my special interest in newborn infants and my experience with a temporarily handicapped baby of my own, all helped to immunize me.

My years off did not begin abruptly. I married during my last term at Simmons, then worked at Children's Medical Center for six months after my graduation. At that point we moved from Boston to California, and I soon found two openings. One was at a community hospital where I would be a staff physical therapist and the other at a private home for severely handicapped children and adults where I would be the only physical therapist.

A kindly local pediatrician attempted to take my career in hand. He invited me to his office to discuss my choice between the two openings and urged me to bring my husband along, apparently to emphasize the solemnity of the occasion. He informed me that because I was at the beginning of my career it was vital that I take the hospital staff job. The home was badly organized, and, if I worked there, I would find myself "hopelessly involved" with the patients.

Although it was not the one he intended, he did make my decision for me, and I never regretted it. There had been no physical therapy program at the home for more than a year, but the equipment was excellent and included a heated pool. The rest was up to me. I had never had it so good.

The place was an "institution," of course, but not the huge, cold prison-like sort. Many of the residents were cerebral palsy victims, some were schizophrenic, and a few more autistic. Some had parents or other relatives who took them home fairly often. Various clubs gave parties, showed films, and took kids on outings. Several college student volunteers helped in the swimming program.

With all this involvement already underway, I had no trouble filling the physical therapy program with children, noise, and laughter. I used utterly "unprofessional" inducements to get things going—balloons, kittens, squirt guns, masks, and anything else interesting that came to hand. For the cerebral palsy patients, who ordinarily experience very little body contact except when being bathed or dressed, I organized wrestling contests. Two days a week became Game Days, with relay races, spelling bees, and dress-up parties, and most staff members soon were taking enthusiastic part. We didn't discuss such staff participation. It just happened.

I did not think of what I was doing as open rebellion against the established way of treating patients in a place like that. If I had planned to stay there more or less permanently, I probably would have been forced to think that way because of the effect on my reputation with the medical establishment. But I was already pregnant when I went to work there and, although I took only a couple of months off before and after the birth of my son, I had to leave when he was six months old to accompany my husband to Kenya where he taught for two years at a school organized by the Society of Friends.

There were many tears when I said goodbye to everyone at the home. Mine were not only for the loss of dear friends; some were for my career, which I knew must now go into what I thought of as storage for at least a few years. As it turned out, it was more like a time of further training of a sort not available in any conceivable school. It was scarcely a kind of training I can recommend to others, but it proved invaluable when I resumed my career.

My daughter, Laura, was born in Kenya. Although we were deep in the back country, I had the help of a well-trained obstetrician and an easy time of it. Laura was a pretty, happy, and firmly self-assertive baby, showing not the slightest sign of any birth defect. She still seemed so at the age of one-and-a-half, but by then I had noticed that she was having a little trouble walking alone. She easily pulled herself up to standing position but would not try launching out on her own, insisting on having solid pieces of furniture or someone's hand to hold onto.

At that point we returned home, and I took her to a pediatrician for a checkup, mentioning the walking problem she seemed to have. He, too, could see no indication of anything wrong but said it might be a good idea to take some X-rays. As I undressed that wriggling little body in the X-ray room, I had a sudden premonition of disaster.

The technician pronounced the first set of pictures no good. I had to plunk Laura back down on the chill, hard table for a repeat. Afterward, it seemed to me that I sat trying to comfort my wailing child for a long, long time before the technician stuck her head in the door and, without looking at me, said: "The doctor wants to see you right away."

It was a moment that only the parents of "defective" babies can fully share with each other.

The doctor met me in the hall and put an arm around me as we walked toward the exit. "Her hips are dislocated," he said. "Must have been born that way. I've made an appointment for you with an orthopedist. He's good. Try not to worry."

I was not too stunned to start blaming myself. How could I have failed to suspect? Was all my training for nothing? What if her hips were too far gone to repair?

During my student years I had seen many children under treatment for congenitally dislocated hips, a misfortune that befalls about one in eighty girl babies and many fewer boys. It is easy to check for and to correct at birth when the hip joints are still soft and cartilaginous. My obstetrician should have caught it. But she hadn't. And I hadn't. And now I kept remembering the children I had seen in whom it was detected at later ages: two-year-olds almost completely encased in plaster casts, six-year-olds in braces and on crutches, adolescents in wheelchairs. I remembered especially the terrified wails of the smallest ones when they recognized the ward where they were to undergo what was for them just more torture.

The orthopedist was of the "cool objectivity" persuasion and said as little as possible. He confirmed the pediatrician's diagnosis and outlined the treatment: hospitalization for three days, general anesthesia to permit him to relocate Laura's hips, then a body cast to cover her from nipples to toes with cut-outs for vital functions. A cast change and more X-rays would be necessary every six weeks. He added that she was close to the two-year borderline. Children in whom the deformity went untreated after that age usually required surgery. He thought we had caught the problem in time to avoid this but could not guarantee it. His final words: "Take her home. Have a good Christmas. And have her at the hospital by four P.M. on the twenty-sixth."

I staggered from his office feeling drained and nagged at by memories of exhausted mothers pushing wheelchairs and lugging suitcases and tattered security blankets in and out of children's wards. Would I ever again wake up and not feel crushed by the thought of Laura's birth defect and its effect on her life? Wouldn't I have to spend most of my time trying to make life in a cast bearable for her, thus turning her into a spoiled invalid who would demand constant attention, dominate the family, and drain off its energy?

And my three-year-old son, Chris. What was Laura's need for so much of my time and attention going to do to him?

And the money. My husband was still looking for a job, and we had no health insurance. How would we ever pay all the hospital bills and physicians' fees? They were bound to run to many thousands of dollars.

And guilt. Had the pills I took for airsickness on the long trip to Kenya affected Laura's fetal development?

If only we had never thought of going to Kenya . . .

If only the obstetrician had checked her hips . . .

If only I had been more concerned about her reluctance to learn to walk unaided . . .

For mothers of babies with birth defects, such agonizing is as inevitable as it is useless. And as so often happens when one settles down to live through agony, we found that our fears were wildly exaggerated. First off, I learned that the school in Kenya had taken out for us a kind of insurance that covered any medical problems showing up within three years after we left there. And then, to my thankful astonishment, Laura took to life in a cast as if it were the natural way to live. When they brought her back to her room after re-setting her hips and molding the cast around her, she was still groggy from the anesthesia, but she looked like a jolly little turtle. And like a jolly little turtle was just how she behaved most of the time during her six months in the cast.

What makes it possible to repair congenitally dislocated hips this way is that up to about two years a baby's hip joint stays more like cartilage than bone. By aligning the legs and pelvis properly and keeping them aligned as bone hardens and the muscles grow, the orthopedist can reshape the joint so that it functions the way it should. In Laura's case this alignment meant holding her legs with the knees wide apart in a way that at first seemed to me impossibly awkward even for a little while and agonizing when kept up for a long time. Laura was so young and supple both physically and emotionally that the position seemed not to bother her at all.

Only a day and a half of hospital observation were necessary to make sure that the cast was working properly, and then I took her home. My husband and I were inspired to make her a little wooden platform on casters. Strapped on it face down so that she could propel herself about with her hands and elbows, she almost immediately started zooming around as if she had been born to that form of locomotion. I made her a whole wardrobe of sweatshirts to protect the skin of her arms and hands because she refused to be confined to indoor scootering. Drivers on our street often took their feet off their accelerators, craned their necks, and stared open-mouthed at the strange sight of me and my little tortoiseshell offspring perambulating our sidewalk.

Even the visits to the hospital every six weeks for new X-rays and changes of the cast did not bother her much. By the time the last cast was removed and replaced by a brace, she had developed a considerable vocabulary. It enabled her to complain about the loss of the cast. Without it, she informed me, her legs felt cold.

Both my early anxious foreboding and the ultimate outcome are typical. Countless parents of handicapped children have assumed, on first discovering the handicap, that it must mean excruciating pain and misery for the child. They have a chance to learn an invaluable lesson from the way the child takes the handicap for granted and makes the most of the situation.

Another part of my experience was not so typical. Still, it is by no means a unique incident. I report it here partly by way of warning to other potential victims of such treatment but chiefly in protest against the way the medical establishment seems almost to encourage self-righteous arrogance.

As I have mentioned, the orthopedist who treated Laura did not from the beginning want to be much involved. He continued coldly businesslike through the first year-and-a-half of her treatment. He either answered my very few and fully winnowed questions with briefness that often seemed rude or, occasionally, simply ignored them and me. But she made such excellent and steady progress—and I had, like most Americans, grown so used to such behavior in medical specialists— that I made do with the few scraps of information he did condescend to toss me.

Then, when Laura had become proficient at walking with the support of her brace in a seemingly awkward but quite successful combination of hop and waddle, my husband and I began considering the possibility of returning to Kenya for another year or two. Our first concern was whether it would be all right for Laura. The orthopedist had assured us that both hip joints were re-forming beautifully, and we knew there were good hospitals and, presumably, specialists in Nairobi. But we had to make sure she could get as good treatment there as at home before we could be really serious about the move.

The next time I took Laura to the orthopedist, he again

assured me that she was doing quite well, so I told him about our thought of returning to Africa and asked how we could find out whether Laura could get any further necessary treatment in Nairobi. His coolly objective manner was replaced by red-faced rage so quickly that for a while I could not take in what was happening.

"I do not know," he said in a voice that was close to a hiss, "what you and your husband think you are doing—teaching savages to wear clothes and read."

He glared at me for a moment, then went on.

"You had better arrange to leave your daughter here with some relative or friend, if you have any. She's going to need surgery. I'll do the left hip first, next month. I'll do the other as soon as she recovers."

I was open-mouthed. "But I thought you said . . ." was all he let me get out.

"The hips are not responding properly. I'll make a reservation at the hospital for as early as possible next month."

With that he got up, stalked out of his office, and slammed the door behind him. It was the last time I ever saw or spoke to him, and I still do not know for sure what it was all about. His problem may have been simple racism or some more complicated kind of ignorant prejudice. I suspect it would have made little difference to him even if I had been able to explain that what my husband taught in Kenya was not the wearing of clothes but the equivalent of junior college English to boys preparing, in many cases, for further study at such universities as Oxford and Cambridge.

When I recovered from the hard jolt he dealt me, I realized that to his mind even his rage and his threat to perform surgery on Laura probably were justified ways of teaching me what he judged to be a much needed lesson. He clearly felt that he was so much better qualified than I that his opinion on anything whatsoever took absolute precedence over my own.

Through a physician friend we found another orthopedist who assured us that Laura's hip joints were coming along beautifully and showed not the faintest sign that they would profit at all from surgery. He took over the treatment, which eventually left her hip joints as good as anyone's. He also found out for us that there were specialists in Nairobi well qualified to follow up if we wanted to go there, though we ultimately decided for other reasons against returning to Africa.

Obviously, I do not mean to suggest that all—or even a great many—physicians are prone to irresponsible behavior. But other parents of handicapped children have told me of enough similar experiences with high-handed specialists to make clear that it is by no means as far out of the ordinary as it should be. More compassionate specialists are aware that there can be problems. A pediatrician I know who works with the families of many children suffering birth defects offers this advice: "If you do not feel that you can communicate well with a physician treating you or your child, there is something dangerously wrong somewhere. The only thing to do is look for another physician."

By the time Laura had progressed to the point of being able to attend kindergarten classes, we were living in a small city, and I took a part-time job teaching at a nursery school which had recently started a program for retarded children between the ages of two and seven. One day I was watching the children with a public health nurse who was consultant to the program. A two-year-old was moving around the room lyng on his back and pushing himself along with his feet.

"If only," I remarked to the nurse, "I had been able to work with him before he got set in that habit."

She told me about a new program she had heard of in which physical therapists were working with handicapped babies as young as two or three months. I was intrigued and asked her to let me know if she ever heard of anything like that being tried in our area of San Luis Obispo, California. A few weeks later she telephoned to do just that and, although I did not then realize it, I had at last found my life's work.

2

Why Not House Calls?
or "There's No Place Like Home"

THAT WAS 1972 and a wonderful time to go back to work
with handicapped children because it was the beginning of the
great change in the approach to them. This change has been
little noticed because it involved nothing easily dramatized by
the media. Indeed, one of the most important factors seems
too crass to even be thought of as helpful to the handicapped:
namely, the clamor against welfare expenditures.

About a century ago California and most other states began
assuming responsibility for the care of the mentally disturbed,
the retarded, and many of those with severe physical handicaps, though the care often amounted to little more than feeding, watering, and cleaning them in huge and crowded institutions. By 1960 both the numbers needing such care and
the cost of providing it were skyrocketing. Objections to the
snake-pit conditions in some of the institutions also were
growing in volume.

It is typical of our American addiction to the technical fix
that most credit for our considerable progress toward solving
those problems is given to the development of drugs for tran-
quilizing inmates displaying difficult behavior. In fact, it was
the change in approach to retarded and physically handicapped children that has been far more beneficial to the recip-
ients and their families. And all that was necessary to make
it possible was a change in attitude.

The old attitude was based on the seemingly obvious fact
that you cannot teach a child anything until it is old enough

24

to understand what you are trying to teach. When I was in training in the late fifties, only a few infants with problems like dislocated hips or polio were brought in for physical therapy. Schools that accepted retarded or physically handicapped children hardly ever took them before the age of six. The idea that physical therapists could help infants in their general physical development simply did not seem to occur to anyone. We dealt only with specific problems such as tightness of muscles around a hip or weakness of muscles of a foot.

In the mid-sixties the clamor against the big institutions led California to organize programs of professional help for handicapped children living at home. The economic argument was that this would help encourage the families of these children to keep them home. One such program took the form of nursery schools for the retarded, which started with a lower age limit of four but dropped it to three when it turned out that the younger ones also could benefit. Next, a few of these schools tried adding physical therapists to their staff. When this worked out well, the idea of having us work with still younger children was suggested tentatively.

That was the point at which I came along. The program in which my nurse friend involved me was new not only in setting no lower limit on the age of the children, but also in including children with any sort of handicap who might benefit from the help a physical therapist could provide. And so one morning in November, 1972, I found myself in a spare room at a state-supported nursery school surrounded by six babies suffering from a startling variety of afflictions and six mothers with long lists of questions, hopes, and fears.

The effect on me was a little like that of jumping into a mountain lake full of water that had been part of a glacier only a little while before. For a moment after I first entered the room I felt paralyzed. And terrified.

The six children ranged in age from six months to two years. All their handicaps were more severe than Laura's had been, but the youngest seemed to me, at that stage in my experience, utterly unapproachable. Born prematurely, she had weighed only three pounds. Her afflictions included congenital malformations of her respiratory system, including a collapsed voice box. She could make no sound and breathed only with the help of a tube inserted through her throat into her trachea. Several bouts of apnea (difficulty with breathing) had kept her in hospitals for most of her short life.

At the opposite extreme was a two-year-old who was spastic on one side and hyperactive. When I arrived at our improvised clinic, he was charging around the room falling over toys and other children and bumping into furniture. His weary mother was pursuing him half-heartedly and ineffectually.

Besides being shocked by the problems these children faced, I also saw myself as an outsider. These six mothers and their children had been meeting once a week for two months with another physical therapist whose place I was taking because she no longer had the time to spare. That made me not only a new kid on the block but also a substitute for someone they had learned to trust. Each of the mothers was the one and only expert on her own child and was coping twenty-four hours a day. Who was I to tell them what to do?

But along with all these fearful negatives went one great positive that eventually overruled them. During my years of training in Boston I had studied for several months in a large hospital clinic for children with cerebral palsy. I had learned to hate the stuffy formality of hospital protocol. Mothers who brought their children in were addressed as "Mrs. ———" and treated like machines to be stuffed with certain information and dismissed at the end of the visit without another thought. Children were deposited on the examining table and forced into a rigid routine of stretching this muscle and relaxing that one, their cries, complaints, and attempts to roll away blandly ignored. Obviously, there was going to be none of that nonsense here.

For here I was on their turf and at their mercy instead of the other way round. Although I did not fully realize it at the time, I knew at some level of subconsciousness that this was the way it should be. Seeing patients only in hospitals or one's office is what makes it possible to treat them as abstractions to be subjected to certain tests and other neatly defined procedures. It is no way to treat a fellow human being, let alone someone who is in trouble and is seeking help from you that you are being well paid to give.

I know that I somehow began feeling my way in this direction that first day, though I certainly did not then articulate anything of the sort even in the privacy of my mind. The attitude of that first group also helped me ease out of the role of rigid conventionality. In the easiest and most natural ways possible they helped me past the feeling of being new and on trial. Already very friendly and supportive toward each other because of their shared experiences as mothers of badly handicapped children, they simply passed that friendliness and support on to me.

They made it impossible for me to miss the all-important point. To each mother, her baby, no matter how severely handicapped, still was above all her baby and therefore to be cherished and cuddled and loved. The way medicine often is practiced today makes it all too easy to ignore the baby and focus all attention on the handicap.

This was one point that became vividly real for me within the first few weeks. It surfaced when a new mother showed up at one of our sessions, bringing along her five-month-old son. Born prematurely and still weighing only four pounds, he also was blind. I held him and talked quietly to him just to get him acquainted with me. He began to coo and wave his hands.

"Oh," I said, quite spontaneously and with no thought of anything but the child in my arms, "he's so cute and responsive."

His mother—young, frightened, and often close to tears—gave me a strange look I could not fathom. But at the next session she explained it. "Nobody," she said, "ever told me my baby was cute before."

His blindness, small size, and other problems had kept not only professionals but also his parents' family and friends from seeing him as himself. I realized that being open, informal, and spontaneous about my own interest in their babies would help break down this isolating effect. I also realized that there was no need for me to try to pretend that I had all the answers or to put on any other kind of professional front.

"I'm new at this," was the essence of what I eventually tried to tell the group. "I spent several years learning ways to help children like yours, but you are the ones who know best what your babies need. The important thing is—what do you think your baby needs that I can help with?"

We talked on and on about their problems and what each wanted for her baby. At first we talked in a group, and then I talked individually with each of them. And within a few sessions we were able to pick effective and realistic goals for each child.

The essence of the difference between mothering ordinary children and those with severe handicaps is the need to make a choice. Babies without handicaps need only love and encouragement to develop naturally at their own rates to their own limits. The handicapped ones need the same love and encouragement—but not to be pushed to do what they cannot do. Absolute limits seldom can be set, but it is vital to work toward clearly realistic goals and to keep the others as hopes rather than expectations.

One mother, for instance, wanted above all that her child should be able to walk normally. April, then eighteen months old, had Down's syndrome, which used to be called mongolism. Her muscle tone was extremely poor, and she could sit up for only a minute or so at a time. I could not be sure how and when she would walk, but I was able to explain in detail what we could do—the mother and I working together—to help April improve her muscle tone and the ability to balance herself. These improvements would give her a far better chance to learn to walk well.

The words "explain in detail" are the heart of the matter. I didn't just demonstrate certain exercises and tell April's mother to make April do them so many times a day and so many days a week. That is what I probably would have done if I had been dressed in a white smock and had received them in an antiseptically barren room in some hospital. I would have done it that way because that's the way it's done in such a setting, and it is very difficult there to see the urgent need—the absolute necessity—to do it more humanely.

To treat the mother of a handicapped child coldly is merely to add to her already overwhelming burdens instead of helping her. The relaxed, informal warmth of the conditions under which we met made it possible for me to realize this. My explanations in detail were not in the form of lectures but give-and-take conversations that went on over many meetings, and I kept the emphasis not on doing exercises and other routines in certain rigidly proper ways but on doing them in ways both mother and child could enjoy.

This helped eliminate a lot of difficult problems. For instance, one of my patients, year-old Susie, was terrified whenever she was placed face down. It was important that she learn to like this position so that she could experiment with overcoming gravity by getting up on all fours to try creeping. Her pediatrician could find no indications of any physical problems to explain her fears. So we tried everything I could think of—toys, movement, the examples of ourselves and other children, and so on. Nothing worked. She just screamed inconsolably until turned over or picked up.

Then one day she and her mother arrived at our meeting place with the latter beaming proudly. "I found the way," she announced. "She doesn't just stand for it. She loves it."

The mother lay on the floor on her back, picked Susie up and placed her face down on top of her. Susie lay quiet for a moment. Then she slowly raised her head and chest, supported herself on her arms, looked her mother in the eye, and smiled. It was a triumph. Soon Susie was able to tolerate lying face down by herself and progress on to the great advance involved in getting up on all fours.

At that point, all concerned, very much including me, simply took for granted that my patients should be brought to me at some place I found convenient. Most of those who pay the fees of health professionals in America today have been so thoroughly brainwashed that they hardly ever think of doing things the other way round. Neither, of course, do we whose convenience is served.

Within a couple of months of getting back to work, I was holding weekly clinics for several groups of mothers and their babies. Now and then someone would be unable to get to the meeting place because of car trouble or such. If the trouble persisted, the only thinkable solution was for someone else to bring them to later meetings.

It was Susie, the baby with the problem about lying prone, who helped me think another kind of thought. Susie's family lived in a remote part of the district, far from the nearest other patient. When her mother's car could not be repaired for several weeks, she had no way of getting to town. Susie had been making wonderful progress, and I began to fear she would lose what she had gained. And that was why the idea of making my first house call occurred to me.

Now it seems absurd, but the fact is I was downright sneaky about it. I told no one at our program's headquarters and swore Susie's mother to secrecy. And then I worked feverishly to find her a dependable means of transportation into town so that I would not have to repeat my indiscretion.

However, I can boast that I snapped out of this attitude fairly soon. Once I had made a trip for Susie, I was able to be more relaxed about doing it for others who could not get into town. I began to notice that I sometimes seemed able to work a lot more effectively in a patient's home.

Then one day I learned that our clinic space in the school was needed as a classroom and would no longer be available to us. The light dawned. It was pointless for my patients to come to me. I must go to them.

My headquarters friends were astonished when I told them this but happily agreed. Finding another clinic location was not going to be easy, and the rent for one was sure to be much more than my travels would cost. The revolution quickly became an accomplished fact.

Soon the advantages of working with my patients in their homes became so clear that I was horrified by the memory of my resistance. In the clinics I had been working out of context. I did not—could not—visualize the place and way the mother would go about trying to follow my suggestions when she got home. When I could see where they led, some of my proposals seemed plain silly.

In other words, my de-specialization continued. When you bear a label like "physical therapist," you inevitably tend to dissociate yourself from or to feel unqualified in trying to help your patients in "nonphysical" ways, though it may not always be altogether clear just what that means. In a hospital or clinical setting you often take for granted that a patient's need for such help, a need which may make it impossible for the patient to use the specialized advice you do offer, will be met by someone else. It was impossible for me take such a narrow view of my function when I worked with a baby and its mother in their home.

I do not mean that I have blithely qualified myself as a psychotherapist and hand out advice right and left. What I do is listen, listen, listen. And on occasion I so far forget my professional dignity as to shed a few tears of sympathy. The twenty-four-hour-a-day, seven-day-a-week mothering of a handicapped infant is a way of life that cannot be lived without occasional tears, and to be joined in them by someone who knows intimately what you are going through can be a great solace, for some the only solace available. And when a family needs material help which the usual social agencies are unable or unwilling to provide, I have found that I have many friends who are truly glad to contribute anonymously.

This close involvement with my patients can be painful, sometimes intensely so. And when problems prove insoluble, they can be depressing. It did not take me long to realize that, if I were to try to be involved for anything like eight hours a day and five days a week, I would not last long.

This is, of course, one of the rationalizations for preaching cool objectivity, though not a legitimate one in my opinion. The kind of emotional exhaustion called burnout does afflict many professionals working with the handicapped, the emotionally disturbed, chronically ill, the elderly, and others in desperate need of help. Those who feel in danger of burning out must find ways to protect themselves, and some degree of withdrawal from contact with demanding patients is indispensable. But cool objectivity often amounts to almost total withdrawal.

A few in the helping professions seem to need only a minimum of withdrawal. Among them are some of my best friends. They care deeply for those they work with, give all they've got to that work, and have little left for any life outside it.

It is an heroic way to live, and it is not for me. I think very few of us are up to it. From the beginning I insisted on working only part-time because I wanted a lot of time for my family and other interests, but it also has proved for me an excellent alternative to cool objectivity. About twenty hours spread over two or three days a week are the maximum time during which I can keep giving what my patients need from me. And that includes a good many hours spent on the inevitable paper work. It also leaves me with plenty of energy to be able to permit invasions of my free time when someone needs emergency help.

I don't mean that I'm prescribing this as the proper length of time for others to work. It is what worked for me and may give others some idea of the possibilities. I think it may be of special interest to other women like me who have devoted a few years to raising children and, finding that overwhelming job almost done, want to go back to work outside their homes but do not need full-time pay. At that stage of life many of us have felt that we are on or near the discard heap, ill-equipped for doing anything really worthwhile. In some social circles this also seems to be the community judgment. In fact, great numbers of us are desperately needed and can find great rewards in the helping professions, often with only a little training or updating of skills learned before or during marriage.

Our willingness and ability to work part-time are special qualifications. So is our experience in raising children, which may be the most helping profession of all. It certainly is the most arduous one. My years of experience in it have been more valuable to me than my formal training in my work with my patients.

Another aspect of my story that may interest many women is that, during the period when I was getting back to my career (though not for that reason), my marriage began breaking up. The time and thought I had to give to my patients was subtracted from what I could devote to being miserable about my own situation. It was a helpful subtraction. The break-up went on over a period of three years, and my work became an indispensable consolation.

By the time divorce papers at last were filed, I felt strong enough to go it alone for the rest of my life, if necessary. I not only felt no need to go seeking a man but looked forward to coping by myself for at least a few years. Perhaps that was why I met my second husband, who is helping me write this book, even before the divorce became final. We spent two years together, making sure we both were able to live not only with each other and my children but also with my work, before we made a formal marriage of it. Now my children are almost ready to leave home, and for both my husband and me, life without my work would seem very strange.

3

Slow Thoughts and Deep Feelings

A Child with Down's Syndrome

My patients have been children with a wide variety of handicaps. I am going to tell the stories of some of those who have moved me most deeply—some of them more or less typical and some not at all so. Their stories are fascinating because in some areas they are far in advance of the rest of us in experiencing the limits of what it means to be human.

One story began with a call from a social worker at the agency for which I'm a consultant.

"I've got a new baby for you," he said. "Down's syndrome. Name is Jason. Six weeks old. He's been back in the hospital on intravenous feeding for a week or so because he hasn't been eating. He's the mother's first child, and she is badly depressed."

I called the mother, Lucy, immediately, told her who I was and that I'd like to see her and Jason as soon as possible. Sounding as though she had long since wept herself dry, she told me that she was not sure he would make it, that he would live to come home from the hospital. I told her that, if she would like me to, I would meet her at the hospital so we could visit him together.

"Would you?" she said with the mixture of astonishment and gratitude most Americans seem to feel when anyone in the health professions indicates willingness to go to a little extra trouble to be helpful.

Next morning I made sure of getting to the hospital before

Lucy and introduced myself to the head nurse on the pediatric ward. She had the good news that Jason had begun to take a bottle the night before. They were going to try discontinuing the intravenous feeding.

The baby lay asleep in the incubator, looking more like a newborn than a six-week-old. His arms and legs were shorter than average and quite thin, but his head was nicely shaped and his body sturdy looking. His color was pink and his skin fair. When he at last opened his eyes and looked at me, I saw one of the most common Down's syndrome traits—the little fold in the skin at the inside corner of the eye. This was what led to the use of the term "mongoloid" for such children. To me his appearance seemed better described as elfin, like that of a baby found under a toadstool in a fairy tale.

Lucy arrived while I was looking at him, and I introduced myself.

"Have you heard?" she asked, momentarily almost excited. "He's been taking a bottle. Looks like he's figured out what he's supposed to do."

She looked at Jason with great fondness. And then, abruptly, her enthusiasm evaporated. She sat down, wept quietly, and seemed utterly alone.

A nurse came in, removed Jason from the incubator, wrapped him in a blanket, and handed him and his bottle to Lucy.

"Would you like to try feeding him?"

Lucy nodded. Jason immediately got the idea and sucked eagerly on the nipple. Soon he was also looking in her face.

"See what he's doing?" I asked. "He's sucking, swallowing, and studying your face all at once. That's a lot for a baby to do after a week in an incubator."

"He does look better today," Lucy agreed in a gingerly hopeful way.

"It has been a rough month for you, I should think."

She nodded.

"Having a sick baby is a frightening experience," I tried, hoping to help her realize her feelings were appropriate for a mother of a newborn with problems like Jason's.

"I haven't been able to think straight since he was born, and now I can't seem to think at all. It's like a bad dream that never ends."

"I know," I said. "Several mothers have told me about that feeling. Things will get better for you."

"Have you seen other babies like him? With Down's syndrome?"

I told her that I worked with several. "Would you like to hear something about them? How they develop as they grow up?"

"Oh my god yes," she almost gasped. "Are any of them walking?"

This, naturally, is a great concern of all mothers of handicapped infants, but that Lucy thought a Down's syndrome diagnosis indicated great doubt that Jason would be able to walk meant she knew very little about it.

"Of course," I was able to assure her. "All those I've seen have started walking before they were two. And all of them have been able to get into nursery schools by the age of three or four. Some are in regular programs and some in special education classes run by the county. I hear we have especially good ones here in this county."

"Oh," said Lucy. I had somehow lost her again. In those days she seldom seemed to escape from depression for more than a few minutes at a time.

Almost everyone has few facts and many misconceptions about Down's syndrome. About seven thousand children displaying it are born in this country every year, but most of us have little reason to take interest in them unless one is born into our own family. Even the names by which the condition has been and is known involve misconceptions.

Langdon Down was a nineteenth-century English physician who in 1866 was the first to describe in print several of the physical traits that make up the group of symptoms, or syndrome, now known by his name. Down himself called the children he described Mongolian Idiots. He mistakenly thought that the extra folds of skin at the inner corners of the eyes were the same as those commonly found in the eyes of Chinese and Japanese. This, he declared, meant that the comparatively low intelligence of such children was traceable to Mongolians among their ancestors.

This is outstandingly silly even among the complicated absurdities racists go in for. Not only are the eye folds different from those common in eastern Asia; they are by no means certain indications that a baby will be delayed in mental development, being fairly common among otherwise quite normal infants. What's more, Down's bland assumption that East Asians are somehow intellectually inferior to Europeans is merely a demonstration of his own profound ignorance. China's civilization is older than and at least as complex as that of any Western nation, and some data suggest that the average intelligence of modern Chinese and Japanese is not merely equal to but perhaps a bit superior to that of Occidentals. (For instance, one study of the intelligence quotient scores of ethnic groups in this country found that Chinese-Americans had the highest average score and Japanese-Americans the second highest.)

But the term Down's syndrome does at least emphasize that there are a number of symptoms involved. At the last count I have heard of, the total was up to ninety-six, though it is not likely that any one individual ever has displayed all of them. Among the more common besides the eyelid fold are a special pattern of creases in the palm of the hand, white spots in the iris of the eye, low muscle tone, heart disorders, short stature, and little resistance to respiratory infections. Any of these may turn up in otherwise normal infants, but several together strongly suggest the presence of an extra chromosome number 21.

This comparatively simple deviation explaining Down's syndrome was discovered in 1959 by a team of three French workers in genetics research. Exactly how the extra chromosome is linked with delay in mental development is not yet known. Chromosomes specifically determine simple features of an individual, such as eye color, but in connection with such complex behavior as is covered by the term intelligence they only set more or less elastic limits to the possibilities for development as the child grows. Some individuals with Down's syndrome are severely retarded, but others are much less so. There are as yet no known upper limits to their possible development. At least one of them has written a charming book, *The World of Nigel Hunt* (Garrett Publications, 1967).

All this was news to Lucy. I let it come out gradually in the course of our first few conversations, and every once in a while some of it seemed to perk her up wonderfully. But she kept sinking back into her depression. I felt sure that getting her started working with Jason was the best way to help her out of it, so as soon as he was settled at home and their pediatrician gave the word I made an appointment to visit them.

She was treating Jason as if he were fragile as crystal, had the house overheated, and the poor child swathed in several layers of clothes. I spread a quilt on the floor, picked him up, and unwound the cocoon. He responded enthusiastically.

"Look at him kick," I said. "He's really giving his leg muscles a workout."

All Lucy could manage was a wan smile. I picked up a rattle and shook it in front of Jason. He turned his head in the direction I moved it.

"He's making a start toward coordinating vision and movement," I pointed out. "That's a big step for a two-month-old."

"You really think he's doing well?" Lucy was obviously skeptical. "He's bound to be a long way behind other babies his age, isn't he?"

This is among the many not necessarily true "facts" everyone knows about Down's syndrome babies. Most of the textbook information and statistics on them were collected in the 1940s in the course of studies of children placed at birth in institutions. They usually were treated like valuable animals, but any affection or encouragement they got had to be volunteered by overworked and underpaid attendants. In such circumstances normal children also would be very slow to learn to sit, walk, use the toilet, communicate, and do anything else well-loved babies learn with ease and pleasure.

I explained all this to Lucy and suggested that the best thing to do was forget about Down's syndrome and concentrate on Jason. We were kneeling beside him when I said this. He looked back at us and smiled so broadly it would have been easy to believe that he understood.

By then I had seen enough of his behavior to suspect that he had to a considerable degree one trait often mistakenly listed as a handicap. This is the looseness of the joints which makes many Down's syndrome children seem floppy. Checking on his range of motion in shoulders, hips, elbows, knees, wrists, and ankles, I soon confirmed this.

"See how far apart I can spread his knees?" I asked Lucy. "And how far back I can bring his arms?"

"It doesn't hurt him?" she protested, anxious as all new mothers usually are until they get the hang of mothering.

Jason's reactions were the only answer necessary. He was gurgling with pleasure.

"I don't want to sound Pollyannaish," I said, "but this is one way some Down's syndrome children have an advantage over other children. There are lots of activities in which flexibility like that will be a real asset—dancing, tumbling, and such. When Jason is older, you may want to think about enrolling him in a dance class."

Lucy laughed for the first time since I had met her, though it was only a tiny laugh.

"Wow. I'll do it. What a day that'll be."

She was really just humoring me, but it felt like a breakthrough.

"Notice how he's squirming around on the quilt," I plunged on. "He likes the feel of it. Our skins are great big sensory organs. For a baby it sometimes seems to me the skin is the all-important sense. If you keep him bundled up, he doesn't get to use it as much as he ought to."

I was concentrating on Jason when I said this and didn't notice the change in Lucy's expression.

"What difference does it make?" she asked in what sounded like a half-strangled snarl. "What good's a sensory organ to him?"

There was nothing I could say, so I sat back on my heels and waited for her to go on. She buried her face in her hands.

"My husband . . ." she said, "we . . . we don't know whether we can . . ."

It is agonizing to watch someone struggle like that and be unable to help actively, but I knew from experience that all she could use of what I had to offer was my attention.

"He's my baby, . . . Oh! He's my baby. I can't . . . I can't . . ."

She sobbed for a few moments.

"But we don't have to decide . . . We can . . . He said any time."

It developed that their pediatrician had told them about the possibility of placing Jason in one of the remaining institutions if he turned out to be so severely handicapped that they, themselves, were unable to cope. Even if the doctor had not mentioned it, the thought of doing it was bound to hover in the back of Lucy's mind. Almost all parents of handicapped infants go through times when their burden seems unbearable.

"I'm sorry," Lucy groaned. "I don't know . . . We don't know . . . Oh, will he ever be anything more than a vegetable?"

For answer I put Jason on his back and leaned over him smiling. Using a soft dry washcloth, I briskly stroked his arms from shoulder to hand, four or five strokes for each arm. I stopped and waited for his reaction. He held still for a few seconds, then slowly flexed both arms at the elbows and shoulders, raised them over his head, brought them quickly back down to his side, and repeated this raising and lowering three more times.

"What made him do that?" Lucy asked.

"Stimulation," I said. "The stimulus to his skin gets passed on to the muscles underneath. Now you try another kind."

I found her a soft hairbrush, turned Jason over on his stomach, and suggested that she stroke from his head down his neck and back.

"Am I doing it right?" she asked the inevitable question.

"Jason is the only one who can tell you. If he doesn't like it, he'll let you know. If he doesn't respond at all, it's probably because you aren't stroking firmly enough. Try different things to stroke with—a piece of fur, a sponge, a wool sock. Do all the experimenting you can think of."

When she finished the back stroking, Jason responded beautifully by lifting his head for a moment.

"I've never seen him do that before," Lucy said.

"You'd seldom see an ordinary two-month-old do it, either," I assured her, "unless someone provided the necessary stimulation. It takes a lot of muscle effort for him to get his head up. He has to work at it."

Jason's response gave me an idea of the best thing for Lucy to start working on with him. As any gymnast or fancy diver can tell you, movements of the head and neck are the leaders in body movements generally. Most of us non-infants take our control of our head and neck movements for granted and the use of these to lead other parts of our bodies wherever we wish them to go. No infants can do so. For them, such control and such use of it has to be learned.

Until they learn it, they are imprisoned far more rigidly than any adult prisoner can be. Newborn babies cannot even look where they want to look, let alone move where they want to go or reach for what they want to grasp. They are trapped in or near the fetal position and can get out of it only briefly and by what amounts to random trials. Small wonder that most of them emit frequent and noisy expressions of rage and fear.

All of us learn control of body movements starting with the head and proceeding downward, a process referred to in the usual Latinate jargon as "cephalo-caudal development." For starters in this game most babies do have certain inborn reflex patterns. When either cheek is brushed, for instance, the head turns in that direction. The pupils of the eyes move toward strong lights. And so on.

In addition, the effects of gravity also push us to experiment with head movement. When a baby is lying face down, for instance, gravity exerts a pull on the muscles of the back of the neck. They respond by contracting. This lifts the head and immediately provides the reward of an interesting change of view. At first the muscles holding up the head tire quickly, and it drops back. But the baby remembers that interesting view and wants more of it. Sooner or later the same automatic effects of gravity or perhaps just random movements will bring it back. For an ordinary child the next step of obtaining it at will, by learning to control the muscles of the neck and upper spine, will soon follow.

For a Down's syndrome baby with low muscle tone, however, it does not follow so easily. That is where a physical therapist can help a willing mother make a big difference. What the baby needs basically is a great deal more than the usual amount of stimulation and encouragement supplied by someone prepared to be endlessly patient.

In addition to the skin stroking, I showed Lucy several ways to encourage and reward his head movements while he was lying on his back or stomach. Other tricks included carrying him with his back resting against her shoulder so that he faced the same way she did and turned with her, or astraddle her hip so that he had to turn sideways to face the way she was going. I also showed her how to reinforce his efforts with praise, smiles, and by rubbing his back when he was making an effort but not when he stopped trying. To help her get organized I wrote several of these suggestions on little cards.

I promised to come back the following week unless she asked me not to. I heard nothing from her and, on the day of my second visit, felt some suspense about what I would find when I got there. The event was a letdown. Everything was exaggeratedly the same as before—the house overheated, Jason swathed into immobility, and Lucy deeply depressed. She remembered that I had promised to come back that day but seemed to remember nothing of what I had shown her. When I got Jason stripped for action, he seemed a little less responsive than before.

"Well," I asked, "how has it been going?"

She didn't look at me.

"What difference does it make?" she finally asked when the silence got to her.

"With help," I said, "I can promise that he will be able to do a lot more than he would without it."

She started to cry.

"Sometimes I wish he'd die," she said. "Without any pain. In his sleep. And get it over with." Tears ran down her cheeks. "Do you think I'm some kind of monster?"

"No, Lucy, I don't. Even ordinary mothers have times when we can't help thinking about how much easier life would be without children. You have so much more to bear that every once in a while you're bound to think of having it all over and done with."

Suddenly, she was angry.

"I didn't say that! You're putting words in my mouth."

For a moment I felt like responding in kind, but I calmed down. It was hardly sensible to expect her to think logically. Anyway, anger was an improvement on depression, so instead of trying to answer her I went on undressing Jason and repeated what I had shown her about stimulating and encouraging head movement.

She stayed huffy through the rest of that session, but resentment was apparently just what she needed because when I returned a week later she had Jason all ready to go to work. As soon as I took off my coat, she spread out the cards on which I had written suggestions.

"I suppose you want me to show you what we've done," she said in a tone that seemed intended to let me know that she had not forgiven me.

Fortunately, I was feeling strong enough to accept the role thrust on me. We went through the work she had been doing with Jason, and I was able to assure her quite sincerely that he was noticeably more responsive than at my previous visit. Then I showed her a few more ways to encourage him to work at controlling his head movements, such as carrying him upright supported as low as possible down his back so that he would have to hold up most of his body by himself.

She was still a little huffy when I left, but she had accepted an invitation which I felt sure would help her past this point. My switch to house calls had had the one disadvantage of keeping the parents of my patients isolated from each other, so I had persuaded them to have occasional evening get-togethers in the home of one or another. Sometimes they have a pediatrician or other specialist give a brief explanation of some point and answer a few questions, and sometimes they just talk among themselves about their fears and hopes and concerns.

Lucy was one of the first arrivals at the group meeting a few days after my third visit to her home. Parents of three other Down's syndrome children were there, and I made sure she met them. She never told me what they said to her, quite possibly because she didn't remember anything specific from their conversations. But they helped her past both her depression and her need to feel angry at someone. No doubt all misery loves company, but in my experience no kind of misery profits from company more than the kind Lucy had been suffering.

We settled down to the long job of encouraging Jason's

"cephalo-caudal development," mostly with variations on the exercises I've described. One that worked quite well was moving a toy or other interesting object back and forth just outside his line of vision. The idea was to get him to try to move his head a little farther each time. If he was really trying but could not quite manage, we would help him. Another was to put one hand under his shoulder blades and raise him to a sitting position, talking to him the while and doing only the minimum necessary with the other hand to help him keep his head in line with his body. Rubbing his stomach, chest, and throat before starting this helped to increase his interest in making the considerable effort involved.

Before long it was almost routine for Lucy to be bubbling with good news when I arrived on my weekly visit.

"Remember how he used to sleep all the time?" she greeted me one morning. "He's been awake for hours and hours every day this week. He keeps cooing. Sounds like a pouter pigeon. Once he raised his arms and looked at his hands and kept turning them so he could see both sides. He was fascinated."

Another time she met me with an excited: "Look!"

She held him upright supporting only his trunk and Jason, his bright blue eyes wide open, held his head erect with not the slightest sign of a wobble.

"He holds it like that almost all the time now," Lucy crowed.

These little triumphs became frequent and inevitably brought up the question of just how delayed Jason really was in this or that respect. I could hardly ever offer Lucy any but a vague sort of answer. In my experience there has never been an infant born with exactly average potentials. Even if there were, its rate of development would depend on how it was treated by its parents and other adults and children with whom it spent its time.

According to authorities on child development, for instance, an average or normal infant is able to hold its head erect for several minutes at a time by the age of four months. So was Jason. Yet I have known infants who could not be classed as retarded but who were not able to do this until six months or later. Although it is impossible to be certain, it seems to me the explanation probably is that the latter got so little stimulation and encouragement that their development was slowed, whereas Jason got so much that his was speeded.

But, of course, there are limits to what stimulation and encouragement can do. Children with standard genetic endowment and no crippling disease or accidents need little more than opportunity to learn to walk by about their twelfth month. Even with us doing everything we could to help him, this was beyond Jason's capacity at that age.

He almost seemed to try to make up to us for his slowness in learning to walk, though, by becoming a supercrawler. He started crawling in his seventh month, first pulling himself around by his elbows, then getting onto his hands and knees and really zooming. Soon he was opening cupboards, emptying dresser drawers, and making life for Lucy a strenuous game of trying to anticipate what he would get into next. As a crowning glory, he made himself the talk of the neighborhood by getting trapped in the bathroom with the help of a towel drawer which he opened and wedged against the door to the hallway. It took a neighbor with a ladder and an eight-year-old small enough and agile enough to climb through the tiny bathroom window to make the rescue.

Still, it probably is a good measure of the delay in Jason's development that he was about four months late in learning to walk. Near the end of his fourteenth month he pulled himself to his feet to reach for something on a chair, let go when he had it in hand, looked scared, and yelled for help before dropping onto his bottom. But with all the blandishments and inducements we offered, it still took him a couple of months more to progress to his first steps hanging onto an adult hand. One more month went by before he could walk all the way across a room alone.

Shortly after that great day, disaster struck. One morning

Jason awoke crying and remained fussy and irritable. When he refused lunch, Lucy thought he was teething, but by late afternoon his temperature was 101°. She took him to the pediatrician, who could find no explanation and told her to give him plenty of liquids and baby aspirin and watch him carefully. By ten that night he was breathing very fast and his skin was dusky. The pediatrician met them at the local hospital's emergency room, and Jason was admitted with a diagnosis of fever—now 104°—of unknown origin.

Next morning chest X-rays revealed pneumonia. For two days he was delirious. Then he went into deep coma. The attending physician told Lucy that he was not sure Jason would pull through.

"I kept remembering," Lucy told me later, "how at first I had wished he would die painlessly and not have to suffer all the humiliation of being a 'mongoloid.' But it was hard to remember what had made me feel that way, what had made me so afraid about what life would do to him. Because by then I knew how much fun he had just playing with his toys. And how much pleasure he could give me just having fun."

Finally, the antibiotics overcame the pneumococci, and Jason emerged from his coma. He came out fighting. When the needle for feeding him intravenously had to be changed, it took two nurses to hold him still while the doctor made the change. Lucy could not bear to stay in the room during this procedure.

"Even with my hands over my ears in the hall outside his room, I could hear him screaming," she tells the story now, quite boastfully. "I knew then that he was going to get well. Those were the yells of a very determined human being."

One point about which Jason was especially determined was his decidedly negative opinion of hospital fare. For five days after emerging from his coma, he simply would not eat. His physicians insisted that he had to be kept in the hospital and on intravenous feeding until he was eating regularly. Finally,

Lucy was inspired to bring him a slice of her apple pie and some potato chips, his favorite foods. When he gobbled them down, she overruled the doctors and took him home.

"At first I was scared about what I had done," she told me. "He had lost five pounds and looked so pathetic. And for quite a while after we got home, he just lay still in my arms and looked around. I walked from one room to another with him to help him be sure about where he was. When we got to the kitchen he started wiggling like mad and indicating that he wanted to be put down. So I put him down. He crawled straight to the refrigerator and banged on its door."

He ate and ate and ate. At first almost any kind of food seemed to please him, but eventually he specialized in yogurt, cheese, and toast in addition to his apple pie and potato chips. It took him only twelve days to gain back the weight he had lost.

His walking was set back a little further, a good month elapsing before he was back to where he had been when the pneumonia struck. But once he was steady on his feet again, he developed an odd and inexplicable habit of climbing onto couches and chairs and jumping off with his knees stiff. He always landed with a jolt and toppled to the floor, but bad bumps and even a couple of black eyes did not seem to discourage him. I tried having him bounce on an inflated inner tube, do squatting exercises, and everything else I could think of to help him get the hang of landing with bent knees. But more than a year went by before he saw the light and started landing easily. I have no inkling why he had trouble acquiring this particular skill. None of the other Down's syndrome children I have known had such a problem. And once Jason got the hang of landing easily, he never to my knowledge went back to his old, stiff-kneed trick.

Being a duly registered and labeled physical therapist, I was not supposed to concern myself about his development of "communicative and social skills," as the jargon has it. But by the time he was two-and-a-half he needed playmates, so I suggested that Lucy and her husband put a childproof fence around their big, grassy back yard and equip it with a slide, swing, sandbox, and other pieces of playground equipment. Other children of the neighborhood soon clamored to play with Jason, and despite the lack of authorization for my help he progressed rapidly in "communicative and social skills."

It was Lucy who discovered this. At first she hovered around the playground, eavesdropping. She could not bear the thought of Jason being teased or mistreated because of his problems.

"I was determined to do something—I didn't know what, just something—to prevent other children from getting in the habit of calling him 'stupid' or 'dummy' or anything like that. When my kid brother was in the third grade, there was a girl in his class he called a 'retard.' It had made her seem to me some sort of monster. Anyone who tried to make Jason seem like a monster was going to have to answer to me. But he cured me. I don't know how he picked it up, but his first two-word sentence was 'You dummy.' For a while there he was trying it out on every child who came to play with him. First time I heard him say it I thought it was going to make me cry, but instead I found myself laughing."

Being able to see the humor in this was a sort of graduation point for Lucy. She had outgrown her need to fight against every indication or reminder of his difference from other children. She could begin to value him for what he is and enjoy him as he is.

Some champions of Down's syndrome children insist on asserting rather strenuously that such children make up for their lower than usual intellectual capacity by a greater than usual capacity for love and other deep feelings. I can agree that Jason and all the other Down's syndrome children I have known have been remarkably affectionate. To be sure, all of them have been on the receiving end of a lot of openly and frequently demonstrated love, so that one cannot say that my observations are anything remotely like scientific evidence.

But neither can one say that matters one whit so far as Jason or any other individual child is concerned. Certainly, his capacity for loving and being loved has gone a long way toward making up to Lucy for her early anguish about his handicap.

My own official role in his life ended when he was three, but I have seen him from time to time and have had several reports from Lucy since then. As it turned out, the county's special education system I had told Lucy about was not as helpful as I had hoped in his case. The bureaucrats who run it wanted to squash Jason into the classification "Trainable Mentally Retarded" because, as one of them put it: "That's the program all our Down's syndrome children go into."

Lucy quite properly rebelled and found a private and cooperative nursery school that was delighted to have him. The school's board even produced a college student who was studying children having special problems and who functioned as an extra unpaid aide three mornings a week at the school, devoting all her time to Jason. One result was that he saw other kids using the toilet and quickly potty trained himself. His language blossomed, too, and it soon developed that his vocabulary was actually a bit better than that of a few of the other children, none of whom was classified as in any way retarded.

How far he will develop and in what ways is impossible to say. He is now approaching his sixth birthday, and there are no certain limits in sight in any direction. Lucy recently adopted my suggestion of enrolling him in a dance class and tells me he is enthusiastic and doing quite well. If it turns out that there is something to my rather offhand suggestion that loose joints can be helpful, he may be pioneering a new specialty for Down's syndrome children.

On his school playground he looks different from the other kids chiefly in being a little better dressed than most, a stratagem of Lucy's that seems to work well in giving him a certain standing. The extra little fold in his eyelid is easy to see if you look for it but doesn't make him stand out. His teacher says he is enthusiastic about school in general and music in particular.

"He's my best singer," she told me, "and he has started making up songs of his own. One of them is 'I have a yellow dump truck.' It's a favorite with the whole class."

So there you are. He may not become a new Cole Porter or Bob Dylan. But then again, maybe he will.

4
Ugly Duckling
A Child with Birth Defects

In many ways Jason's problems were typical of those of handicapped infants in general. There was, for instance, no hint of anything wrong until he was born. It then at once became obvious that he had difficulties that fitted a well-known pattern. It was clear that neither medical nor surgical intervention could do anything about these difficulties. It also was clear what kind of help he could use to realize his potentials.

Karen's story is different in every one of these respects.

When her mother, Pam, married, she was twenty-eight years old. She and her husband, Tom, worked together in a local business firm. An early start on a family was what they both wanted, and within less than three years they were the frequently exhausted parents of two healthy and active sons. Late in her first pregnancy Pam temporarily retired from her job, making sure that all concerned understood that the retirement was strictly temporary, and when their younger son started nursery school, she began organizing their household so that she could go back to her career.

At that point she discovered she was pregnant for the third time. For a while she felt a little disappointed about the change in her plans, but she soon decided that she would devote herself entirely to enjoying the pregnancy. Tom was delighted that she felt this way, and they began assuring each other that they were going to have a girl this time.

Pam's obstetrician was all in favor.

"For a third pregnancy," he assured her, "thirty-four is a fine age. You look terrific. You're far healthier than any horse I've ever known. Come back and see me every month or so, but it'll be mostly for my benefit. It's a pleasure just to look at you."

Pam enjoyed spreading the news among their families and friends. Then she turned to painting her sewing-room-about-to-be-nursery beige pink—"quite superstitiously hopeful that this would help us get a girl." And she went to work on maternity dresses which she knew from experience she would be wanting by the fourth month. Life was wonderful.

And then it wasn't wonderful any more. One week toward the end of the third month of her pregnancy she awoke on three different mornings remembering a nightmare about being handed her baby wrapped in a blanket. Each time she was too frightened to unwrap it.

Telling me about this later, she said it had been easy for her to think of rational explanations for these sudden fears. For one thing she once had read and been impressed by a magazine article about the comparatively high frequency of birth defects in the babies of older mothers, although the article emphasized that this primarily meant mothers over forty. Also, a few months earlier she had heard about the birth of a baby to a friend of a friend in which the baby's brain was damaged during delivery. And there had been a column in the local paper about pesticide residues on supermarket produce and their possibly catastrophic effects on a fetus.

Pam talked with her obstetrician, and he assured her that her nightmares were perfectly normal.

"I hear that sort of thing three or four times a week," he told her. "There is absolutely no indication of anything wrong. If there were, I'd be doing everything I could about it right now. Just try not to let your worries get you down. But if they do, give me a call. I'm here to help."

For a few weeks after that Pam felt better, the fear no more than an occasional vague uneasiness. When she noticed the baby moving for the first time, the feeling brought her great relief. She got her sons a book, *So You're Going To Have a Baby Sister or Brother*, and kept bringing up the subject in her conversations with them.

Another nightmare abruptly ended this phase. In the dream the baby was born "disassembled." Pam had to put the parts together and kept fumbling with them. She slept no more that night and very little in the two following ones. What she felt was not fear but absolute certainty that something had gone wrong.

When she at last called her obstetrician, her weeping made her incoherent. He told her to come straight to his office, gave her a cup of tea, calmed her, and listened attentively to her story.

"All right," he finally said, "I'll arrange for an amniocentesis. I wouldn't want to do it for every woman anxious about her pregnancy, but I think for you it will mean a much better pregnancy if we do it and you can relax with a good report."

He explained that she would have to go to a hospital in a nearby city where a specialist would take a tiny sample of the amniotic fluid in which the baby was floating. A four-week study of the sample would make it possible to detect any of the more likely genetic defects.

Agreeing to this immediately, Pam was off to the city a few days later. The people who performed the procedure were highly experienced at it and made it almost painless. Even the four-week wait for results was not too bad because she felt that at least something was being done. And the results turned out to be as reassuring as possible. There was no indication of anything the least bit wrong with the baby's genetic equipment.

Tom had been depressed by Pam's fears and was elated by this report. Pam had to pretend a little, but she did feel a bit better. No matter what anyone said, she knew there was something wrong, but she felt that, since it was not genetic, it could be corrected. From then on she kept her fears to herself and lived for the day when the baby would be born and ready to receive whatever help it needed.

Her water broke four days after her due date, and Tom bundled her off to the hospital a little before midnight when her contractions were coming every seven minutes. On arriving she was wheeled straight to the delivery room. She felt even more calm and confident than she had at her first two deliveries. This baby needed help, and the time when she could provide that help at last was at hand.

As the baby's head slid into the obstetrician's hands, Pam heard him breathe an involuntary, "Oh, no."

"What is it?" she asked. "Tell me. Please."

"A little problem, Pam. But nothing that can't be fixed," he said. "Push—now—once more."

There was a pathetic little cry and, for Pam, a tremendous feeling of relief. There was also a great deal of silence in the room. It was so still that Pam easily heard the doctor's soft whisper to the nurse: "Get Campbell."

"Tell me," Pam insisted. "Everything."

"Easy, Pam," he said, wrapping the baby in a large white blanket. "It's a girl—she's a little one—and she's having some trouble breathing. Probably mucus. Ah, here's Campbell."

A man entered, looked at the baby, picked her up, and hurried out with her.

"Who's he?" Pam asked.

"Dr. Campbell, our neonatologist," said the obstetrician. "Specialist in newborns. Don't worry. He's a very good man, and he'll get the breathing problem solved in a hurry."

"What's the other problem you were talking about? Tell me. Now!"

"I'm—I'm—she's got a cleft lip, Pam. And I'm sorry—I think there's a cleft palate, too. It looks much worse than it is. There are excellent results surgically these days. It can all be fixed within a few months. And the . . . I . . . I"

Pam felt sorry for him. She knew that there was far more

than a mere cleft palate wrong with her daughter, but she could wait to learn the whole truth. Anyway, she was exhausted and empty. When the specialist returned and said he was putting the baby in an incubator with a little extra oxygen because of her breathing difficulties, Pam just nodded acceptance.

Later, she awoke briefly to find herself in a private room and Tom sitting beside her holding her hand. Two nurses solemnly wheeled in the incubator, said they could leave it only a few minutes, and tactfully went back out. Tom looked and wept soundlessly. Pam saw the wrapped baby of her nightmare and the cleft lip and a tiny tag of flesh where the right ear should have been. But she didn't weep. She felt that she had passed that stage long since. She drifted off to sleep again.

Next morning hospital nonsense took over for a while. She was awakened at seven to be asked whether she wanted breakfast, which she emphatically did not, and a little later to have her temperature taken. But when she gave up trying to sleep and asked to see her baby, that was pronounced out of the question. Instead of getting mad, Pam had a private fit of the giggles at the absurdity of it all.

Fortunately, she was past that stage when Tom arrived. He had been trying to tell their sons about their baby sister's problems, and he looked woebegone.

"They wanted to know," he said, "do you still want to call her Karen Elizabeth?"

"Of course. That's the name we decided on. Have you thought of something else?"

"No, but I thought that since she has . . . since she isn't . . . Well, I just thought you might want to think of another name."

"Well, I don't," Pam was quite emphatic. "Her name is Karen."

At this point Dr. Campbell and the family's pediatrician

walked in, looking very solemn. Tom stood beside Pam and held her hand.

"Well," said the pediatrician, "we have examined her thoroughly. I understand you know about her cleft lip and palate and her right ear. I'm sorry to say there are other problems. From what I know of you, I'd judge you want to hear about them now and in detail?"

Assured he was right, he took a deep breath and plunged. Karen's left leg was shorter than the right one and her buttock muscles almost nonexistent. Her hands were tightly fisted with the thumbs tucked inside and some of the fingers webbed together. She had a heart murmur indicating some sort of defect in heart structure or function. All these problems together with her breathing difficulties and her small size—at four pounds she was three pounds smaller than the usual full-term baby—suggested there might be many other things wrong with her digestive system, her kidneys, and other internal organs. Worst of all, her brain might have failed to develop properly or there might have been some damage to it. Finally, the two specialists were agreed that she might not live long and probably would need hospital care for as long as she did live.

Pam stayed dry-eyed through all this. Her optimistic feeling that she could at last do something to help her daughter was badly shaken, but it was not completely destroyed.

"I fought like hell," she told me later, "to stay hopeful. I just decided that it was my right to feel that way and that nobody had the right to stop me. For a couple of days I had to pay for the hope with occasional weeping fits, but I didn't mind the price."

At the end of the third day the neonatologist told her that, to his surprise, Karen seemed to have outgrown her breathing troubles and was being removed from the incubator. Pam immediately started campaigning first to hold her baby in her arms, then to feed her, then to take her home. At every stage the physicians resisted because of their fear that Karen might at any moment develop new and dangerous problems. Pam persisted. She at last won grudging permission to take the baby home when Karen was two weeks old.

By then a tiny scraping of tissue from Karen's skin had gone to genetics laboratory. Her various disabilities fitted no known pattern, but the specialists still thought it likely that some sort of mishap involving her genes was responsible for them. A direct study of her tissue would be a much more thorough check on this than amniocentesis could be. Pam knew that they felt it misguided of her to get strongly attached to her baby before the report came through, because for them there was every indication that she would live only a short time and be in frequent need of emergency life-saving measures.

The start of my involvement with an infant patient is supposed to be only through channels. When a newborn has problems with which I might be able to help, the hospital or pediatrician usually informs the agency that contracts for my services, and a professional social worker looks into details and lets me know if and when the agency wants me to call the parents. Pam called me direct when Karen was about three weeks old. She had gotten my name from a friend of a friend whose child I had worked with briefly a year earlier.

"I'm not sure what you can do for Karen," she said after briefly describing some of her muscle problems, "but will you come and see her?"

I said yes, of course, and left the bureaucratic details for later. But when I got there, I regretted for a moment that I had not hidden behind those details. Karen simply stunned me. As I sat looking at her and listening to Pam's outline of her heart murmur and other possible internal defects, I had to fight back tears.

To get myself back on an even keel I concentrated on her hands, which were tightly fisted with the minute thumbs tucked inside. On the right hand all but the little finger were webbed together, and on the left the index and second finger were webbed. By working my little finger inside the fist I was able to help Karen open up one hand at a time. I showed Pam how to do this and how to stretch the thumb and roll it so that it faced the palm.

It was sadly little to offer, but it was at least something. I wanted to help Pam do what she could for Karen. On the other hand, I did not want to do anything to build up her hopes in what might be a hopeless situation. I knew it was quite possible that Karen's combination of physical handicaps would be accompanied by mental retardation, perhaps severe. Still, if she could use her hands, her life—if she were to have any life at all—would have a lot more to it.

In any case there was nothing more I dared do at that point. The heart murmur might indicate a defect that would make dangerous any exercises for her trunk or arms or legs. I explained to Pam the reasons for proceeding cautiously and promised to confer with her pediatrician as soon as he could see me.

Arranging that took a few days, and by the time I saw him he had examined Karen again. The heart symptoms had improved a bit.

"By all means do what you can," he told me. "It won't be much, but Pam needs all the help she can get from people who are realistic about the situation. We'll know more when we get the results of the chromosome study. In the meantime you can at least help Pam feel she's doing something for her baby. She's obsessed about that."

He was right. I saw them the second time a few days later, and Pam told me she had been working with Karen's hands the way I had showed her for five minutes out of every waking hour. I had suggested that as a maximum when she had asked how often she could do it. It had been an offhand suggestion. I realized that I was going to have to be very careful about my recommendations.

But Pam had gotten good results. At Karen's age of four

weeks all babies' hands are lightly fisted most of the time. Except for the webbing, Karen's now were almost normal, the fisting much looser and the thumb outside quite frequently.

Pam did not know that this was a big improvement and was disappointed that she could not get Karen to keep her hands open all the time. When I explained, she was jubilant. The slightest encouragement was like water in the desert for her.

To see how much Karen could uncurl from the fetal position, I picked her up, cuddled her for a moment, put her down on her back, then pulled her up by her arms to a sitting position. Her head lagged behind her trunk for a moment. Then she lifted it upright. The corners of her poor, misformed mouth turned up a little.

"Look!" Pam almost shrieked. "Look! She's smiling."

That put me in a bind. On the one hand her hopes seemed on the point of zooming out of sight. Smiling is uncommon behavior in even a physically perfect four-week-old, and I felt sure that the condition of Karen's mouth made possible many other explanations for the way the corners of her mouth had turned. On the other hand, Pam needed consolation. I simply could not bring myself to tell her that I had once worked with a child who at four weeks often seemed to smile but who later proved to be severely retarded.

"Well," I said, "it certainly looked like a smile."

Out of the corner of my eye I saw Pam look at me sideways and give a little shrug. I was surprised by her finding it so easy to calm down, but since she said nothing, I went on testing the muscles and tendons in Karen's neck and upper torso. They seemed to be all present and in working order but noticeably weak. Since there seemed to be nothing I could do about the buttock muscles or shortened leg for the time being, I worked out some simple exercises for her upper torso and showed Pam how to put her through them.

My next few weekly visits were routine. Pam kept up her work with Karen's hands and shoulders, and all seemed to go well. The surgical verdict was that Karen's lip and palate should be repaired first and the freeing of her fingers left until later. Since the mouth work was not to be done until she was three months old, she had to make do with webbed fingers for the time being, but they seemed not to bother her much. That helped me feel some satisfaction about having been able to help her unclench those tight fists.

Inevitably, once the approximate time for the mouth operation was set, we all tended to invest a lot of our hope for Karen in it. The reactions of those who came in contact with her reinforced this tendency. Most of the family's friends took one look, if any, and thereafter behaved as though Karen were so great a catastrophe that the only thing to do was to ignore not only her but also Pam and Tom.

This shrinking away is, in my experience, the usual reaction of friends of the parents of badly handicapped babies.

"I just don't know what to say," is the gist of the self-justification I have often heard. "What can anyone say about anything as awful as that?"

If any readers want my advice about such a situation, it is: "Above all, *don't* shrink away."

Parents of infants with problems do need a lot of privacy, of course, but they also sometimes desperately need friends with whom they can talk about their troubles and from whom they can hope for sympathy and, occasionally, more tangible help in the way of volunteer baby sitting.

Strangers are another matter. The sudden and unexpected sight of a disfigured infant seems to produce barbarically unfeeling reactions in some people. Pam told me of an incident that occurred in a supermarket. She had dressed Karen in pink gingham with matching sunbonnet and was wheeling her in the cart down an aisle when a rather ugly woman she had never seen before leaned over and lifted the edge of the bonnet so that she could admire the baby. She quickly drew back and for a moment stood rigid.

"How dare you?" she gasped. "How dare you bring anything so ugly in here? You should keep it home."

Pam was first astonished, then infuriated.

"You look pretty awful yourself," she said. "Why don't you take your own advice?"

She laughed about it when she told me this story.

"When I calmed down, I was sorry I had been so sharp with her. The operation is going to make Karen look fine, and there's no operation that can do anything for that poor woman's looks. I guess the sight of Karen gave her a bad scare."

Fear does, I suspect, account for most such reactions to babies with physical deformities. But at least we have progressed a little since the good old medieval days when anyone with a visible handicap was likely to be judged out of favor with God and thus a suitable subject for tormenting.

At last the report from the genetics laboratory came through. There was absolutely no sign of anything wrong with Karen's genes. Of course, human genetic equipment is almost inconceivably complex, and we are a long, long way from full understanding of it. Still, the report does suggest that some sort of outside influence might explain what happened to Karen in the course of her growth in the womb. Pam never had smoked, and while carrying Karen she drank not even so much as a glass of wine nor more than a cup of coffee or tea a day. She took no drugs at all, not even an aspirin, nor had she suffered so much as a cold in the way of illness during pregnancy. Since even tiny amounts of such chemicals as pesticide residues in a mother's food and any of several air and water pollutants can affect the development of a fetus, these could explain what happened. In the present state of medicine and the law, however, these can only be possibilities which there is no way of pinning down.

What made Pam feel so sure during the pregnancy that something was going wrong also remains a mystery. We talked about it a few times, and she could never say more than, "I just knew."

She also "just knew" that Karen eventually was going to be all right. By the time the baby was three months old and went off to a big city hospital for the operation to repair her lip and palate, she was at least not as badly off as had been feared at first. None of the problems with her kidneys or digestive system, which the specialists had anticipated, had actually developed. Also, she seemed to have outgrown whatever had caused the heart murmur.

While the family was gone, I called the pediatrician, told him I was beginning to feel more hopeful about Karen, and asked his opinion.

"Well," he said after a brief silence, "you're getting involved pretty deep. I guess I had better tell you. A few years ago I had a patient, a boy with several of the same problems as this child. By the time he was nine months old his skull was developing gross asymmetry. We eventually determined that most of his brain tissue simply had not developed. He had an IQ of less than ten, I think it was. The family moved away, but I've heard that they put him in a state hospital for custodial care."

It was a quietly effective little speech and left me stunned. I understood that he was painting the darkest possible picture of Karen's future in order to keep me from getting too hopeful and making Pam the same. He was so successful that, when Karen came back from the hospital, the red scar where the split in her upper lip had been repaired seemed to me almost as disfiguring as the split, even though I knew from past experience that the scar would gradually fade close to invisibility.

Disfigured or not, however, Karen's repaired lip did turn up at the corners quite frequently in unmistakable smiles when anything pleased her. And a great many things seemed to please her now. I simply ignored the question of how this could fit in with a diagnosis of severe retardation and concentrated my attention on her hands and on helping her get control of her head and trunk.

She responded enthusiastically to skin stimulation and to little stratagems for getting her to track moving objects by holding up her head and swiveling it around. And then, all on her own, she took to rolling from side to side, while lying on her back. She seemed to be doing it just for fun, so I experimentally helped her roll all the way over by turning her underdeveloped hips while she used her much stronger shoulder muscles. She made clear that she enjoyed this, so I built a little ramp by propping up one end of a piece of plywood so that it was about six inches off the floor and covered it with a thick quilt. Putting her on her back at the upper end, I encouraged her to roll sideways downhill, keeping my hands on her lightly in case she got scared. She showed no sign of fear and gurgled with pleasure.

As it happened, I had only a couple of sessions of this work with her after her mouth operation before a series of chances and mischances (she had a slight strep infection, I was out of town for a meeting, and so on) kept us apart for a month. Pam went on working with her, of course, so I was full of curiosity about the changes I would see when at last we got together again.

By then Karen was five months old. Although still small for her age, she had grown unmistakably since our last meeting. She received me enthroned in her infant seat at the kitchen counter.

"Good morning, Karen," I said. "Feeling good? Ready to go to work?"

She looked intently and quite solemnly at me for a moment, then broke into a wide smile and started talking. It was her own private language, of course, but it was unmistakably addressed to me and intended to inform me about something of importance.

"Ah ba-wa ah-ah bwa-ah wah-ah-da ah ah."

"Really?" I said. "Tell me more."

And she did, at great length. One of her "sentences" lasted fifteen seconds. I happened to time it on the kitchen clock behind her. That's how long it takes to repeat the first sentence of the Gettysburg Address.

"Absolutely flabbergasting," I said to Pam. "How long has she been doing this?"

"Doesn't seem very retarded, does it?" she replied with a grin.

"Retarded? Who told you she's retarded?"

"Well, nobody actually said the word. But I know the pediatrician thinks she may be—or anyway, he's afraid she'll turn out to be. And you do, too, don't you?"

She had me. There obviously was no point in being anything but honest with her. I could not discuss what the pediatrician had told me, but my own opinion was mine to do with as I chose.

"My question first," I said. "How long has she been doing this?"

"I think the first time she seemed to be trying to say something was when we got home from the hospital after the mouth operation. She has been doing it more and more often ever since."

"So she was about three months old when she started," I said. "Well, that's the earliest age at which babies do much babbling. Many don't get started until they are four or five months old. I just don't see how a *severely* retarded child her age could do what Karen just did. It was a kind of super-babbling. But with all the problems she has, you just have to know about the possibility that she may turn out to be at least a little delayed in her development."

"Now that's what I call a judicious statement," said Pam with a little laugh. "And it's fair enough. I know you're trying to keep me from setting myself up for a bad time later on. But don't worry. I'm willing to take the chance. It's my decision, and I'll take the consequences."

After that I buckled down to work on what I could see and tried to ignore the whole question of Karen's mental development. Her hands, thanks to Pam's dedicated efforts, already were distinctly more than the mere clubs they would have been without regular work on them. In fact, they were good demonstrations of how great a difference physical therapy can make for an infant somehow prevented from developing in the usual way.

We tend to take our hands for granted unless something happens to them. If you want to get the feel of how important they are to you, try keeping your fists clenched for a while. That makes it difficult to do even something involving so little apparent physical effort as reading a book. Really tight fisting of the kind Karen was born with can make it almost impossible to do so much as wash the palms and the inside of the fingers.

But Pam's success in getting and keeping Karen's fists open was only a beginning. Besides having some fingers on both hands webbed together, Karen had very weak thenars, the muscles that bulge out at the bases of normal thumbs. It's with these muscles that we move our thumbs around in opposition to the fingers. The ability to do this is what makes human hands such versatile tools. Without good thenars all you can do with your thumb is pinch the side of it against the side of your index finger as you might pinch together the jaws of a pair of tongs.

When she was about six months old, a local surgeon was to perform the minor operation of cutting away the skin that webbed together Karen's fingers. In preparation for that day Pam and I worked to build up the strength of her thenars and her interest and skill in making what use she could of her hands. We kept inserting the handles of rattles and other noisy and colorful toys between her thumb and index finger. Soon she got the idea and began grabbing lobster-like at anything that interested her. To make her aware that there is a better way to do it when you can, Pam several times a day would rotate Karen's thumbs around so that they faced the index fingers and press the tips together.

Our work on her trunk control helped with this, too, because it strengthened her shoulder girdle, which has to be stable and strong to make possible good use of the hands. We tricked her into doing little push-ups by putting her prone on the floor and holding interesting items just above her eye level until she pushed her head and shoulders up off the floor to get a better look. Eventually, she was raising not only her chest but also her tummy.

The payoff was great. She had to spend twenty-four hours in the hospital for the hand operation, was completely healed within a week, and was able to hold brightly colored pieces of paper pinched between the sides of her thumb and index finger within moments after the last bandage came off. A few days after that we watched her raise her head and chest from the prone position, support her weight on one hand, and reach for and pick up a toy with the other hand, this time using the index and second finger as tongs. And then one morning Pam called me to report in great excitement that Karen had been sitting in the corner of the couch when a feather floated down onto her lap. She had studied it for a moment, then reached out with her right hand and neatly picked it up with the tip of her thumb swiveled around toward the tip of her index finger. It was a big step forward.

Like her thumb muscles, Karen's buttocks were flat, and the muscles of her short left leg were noticeably smaller than the muscles in the other leg. It was and is possible that some of the muscles just were not and still are not there. The only thing for me to do to help her was strengthen and even over-develop—in the manner of pumpers of iron—what muscles were present.

No infant can be persuaded to do leg lifts or other such exercises, of course, so we had to experiment with a variety of ways of getting her to move her legs around. One she went for was being held by the shoulders in a warm tub of water while gentle jacuzzi action tickled her. The water made her legs so light that she could at last experience the pleasure of kicking out. At the beginning her buttock muscles were so weak that she could move her legs only slowly and gently even in the water, but after a couple of weeks of tub workout three or four times a day her kicks were noticeably more vigorous.

We went on to tying bells and other noise makers to her shoes so that she got interesting results from kicking out as she lay on her back in her crib. A toy that honked when she bumped it with her feet worked similarly. Using a big, soft towel as a sling, I put her on it face down, her head and arms hanging out one side and her thighs and legs the other, and swung her gently back and forth. It made waving her legs around irresistible. She would keep on waving them for as long as my strength held out.

Pam invented other gimmicks. One was a miniature playground slide made simply by tipping up one end of a well-padded ironing board. Karen took up sliding down it head first and would try to look up to see where she was going and at the same time try to lift her legs. This produced beautiful hip extension. Bouncing around on a water bed also delighted her and kept her trying out new kinds of movements of her legs.

All this activity soon inspired her to try moving around a little under her own power. As with many infants, the flat-on-the-belly commando crawl was her first choice. Usually, she got traction by digging in her elbows like oars, but every once in a while she would shove with one knee or the other, proof that her buttock muscles at last were getting strong enough to be of use to her. To test this further I tried holding her in a sitting position on a quilt on the floor, then slowly withdrawing my support. Within a week or two she was able to sit alone for a minute or more, then lower herself back down to the floor.

One morning when she was about eight months old Pam and I were watching her play with some toys on the floor. Suddenly, she pushed the toys away and commando crawled over to the sleeping family cat, known to everyone as Kitty-Kitty. For the very first time Karen got up on her hands and knees, looked down at the cat, and said quietly but distinctly: "Kitty-Kitty."

That was, to put it mildly, an exciting moment. As the books will tell you, most children say their first meaningful words at some point between nine months and a year old— meaningful in the sense of specific and appropriate to the object or occasion. "Kitty-Kitty" was unmistakably specific, appropriate, and a good month ahead of even the early schedule.

Getting up on hands and knees for the first time at eight months, however, is a bit late. Most children do this in their sixth or seventh month. In this sort of skill Karen's physical problems obviously were holding her back. I did not see how it could be thought that anything whatsoever was holding back her mental development.

In the next few months she had many ups and downs but generally progressed on all fronts. She was growing fast and no longer seemed tiny, just a bit small for her age. Nearing her first birthday she had a vocabulary of ten words or more, including "Whazzat?" Often she seemed to use this just as an expression of interest or surprise, but sometimes it seemed unmistakably a request for information.

She was getting steadily more adept with her hands, and it was difficult to detect that there ever had been anything wrong with them. Her lip scar was fading fast, and her hair had grown long enough to hide the fact that her right ear was partially missing. Although she would only occasionally get up on all fours, and continued to prefer the commando crawl for getting around, her buttock muscles were visibly increasing in bulk.

Unlike most handicapped babies Karen stayed quite healthy, catching not so much as a cold for a long stretch of months. For this reason and because he was away for a few weeks taking a refresher course and was then loaded with work on his return, her pediatrician did not see her for several months. She was due for a checkup on her first birthday, and I began secretly imagining the amazement and embarrassment about his pessimism with which he would respond to her. To my delight, Pam asked me to go with her on that momentous occasion because Tom was going to be away at a convention.

Three days before the date, she telephoned me. She was crying.

"Nothing's wrong, nothing's wrong," she hastened to assure me. "But she did it. She stood up."

Pam had been working in the kitchen when she heard Karen call "Mama—Mama" in a terrified tone Pam hadn't heard before. She ran into the living room and found Karen standing at the bookshelves holding on with white knuckles.

"I had to pry her fingers loose. She was in terror of falling. And no wonder! To get up like that she had to make her leg lengths equal by sticking the long one way out to the side. What an accomplishment! And all by herself."

"What a birthday present for you," I said.

Pam giggled. "Maybe she'll walk into the doctor's office."

The visit was a triumph. When the doctor walked through the door of the examining room, Karen pointed at him, frowned, and said, "Whazzat?" While he examined her, she grabbed at the pen in his shirt pocket and screamed an imperious "No! No!" at anything she didn't like, such as having her ear poked into.

When the doctor finished his examination, Pam moved to a chair in the corner of the room and told him to put Karen on the floor. Karen looked surprised when he did so, then glanced around, located Pam, crawled over, and pulled up to standing by holding onto Pam's legs. She managed to balance herself by keeping her longer leg out to the side and a little behind her. The doctor sat on the table and shook his head.

"My god," he said, "I can hardly believe it."

"She says twelve words regularly," Pam boasted, "and tries out one or two new ones almost every day."

"She can kneel for five minutes and work with both her

hands," I joined in, "and she can commando crawl twenty-five feet."

"She points to her eyes, ears, nose, or mouth when you ask her to."

"She puts her doll to bed and covers it with a blanket."

"She uses a spoon and fork."

"She loves to look through picture books."

His head swiveled back and forth between Pam and me as we recited this litany. It was as if he were watching a tennis match. I began to laugh, and so did Pam, and so did he.

"Incredible," he said. "I thought it would take a miracle to make it possible for her to do any of those things."

We talked about her remarkably good health and her remaining problems. He told us that the missing outer ear could be built up with transplants from other parts of her body when she was six. The thumb muscles, so far as he could determine, were developing nicely just with use. How far her buttock muscles would develop, he could not say, but he thought it unlikely that they would ever cause her any walking problems.

"What about the short leg?" asked Pam. "Is it possible it might catch up all by itself?"

"It's possible," he agreed. "With this child, there's no ruling out anything. I think we ought to get her a built-up shoe for now, though, so she can go on learning to walk."

"Is there any operation that might help if the short leg doesn't catch up?"

"Oh, yes. When she's twelve or thirteen, we can operate to stop the growth of the longer leg and let the short one catch up. In fact, every single one of her problems now looks like it can be solved. Or will solve itself."

"Do you think she's retarded?" Pam abruptly asked. "At all?"

He shook his head. "Looking at Karen's developmental skills, I see a typical year-old baby."

I'm sure he thought this a handsome pronouncement. Actually, it has proved to be more like a grudging admission. Not that I blame him. At that point he had not seen enough of Karen to realize what was going on.

On the way home from that appointment Pam stopped at an orthopedic shoemaker's shop and had Karen measured for shoes. When I arrived for my visit a couple of weeks later, she was sitting on the floor and wearing her new foot gear. She immediately crawled over to me on her hands and knees, pulled herself to standing with the help of my leg, and took my hand and tugged to indicate that she wanted to go cruising.

Since then my role in her life has dwindled steadily. All Pam has needed from me has been an occasional suggestion about exercises or activities to try. But as with all healthy children, Karen's own natural programming has kept her finding new things to do for herself to strengthen muscles that need strengthening and improve skills that need improving.

From cruising around while holding onto someone's hand she soon went on to walking unaided from one support to another several feet away, and then without any need of supports to aim at. When she was fifteen months old, she was completely confident on even ground, and we tempted her to try difficult footing such as thick foam rubber and pillows. She loved the challenges and soon insisted on trying her skill on a steep and bumpy hillside nearby. Then she took up dancing, bouncing, and climbing onto chairs and jumping off. By eighteen months Karen had no sign of a limp or other problem in doing anything she wanted to do on her feet, and although her buttock muscles still looked a little small, they seemed quite strong enough for anything she cared to do.

To help her keep strengthening her shoulders, Pam set up a little trapeze in a doorway and taught her to wheelbarrow around on her hands while someone held up her feet. This sort of thing, plus puzzles to manipulate and beads to string, has made her more adept than average in the use of her hands. Not long after her second birthday she took up crayons and produced a readily recognizable masterpiece known in the household as "Tree with Mommy Sitting Under It."

At this writing Karen is a little past her third birthday, and I have become a friend and admirer rather than a therapist. She is a lively and pretty little girl and a wonderful antidote to the glooms that inevitably beset, on occasion, anyone in the health professions who has to deal with hopeless cases. I marvel whenever I remember how nearly hopeless so many of us once felt about her and how magnificently and successfully determined Pam was not to share that feeling.

But as I have hinted, Karen's development has not stopped at the stage her pediatrician assessed as "typical." Not long ago she brought her mother two picture books she had been looking through. She had one of them open at a page with a picture of a cat with the word "cat" in large letters under it and the other at a picture of a cow with the word "cow" under it.

"Mommy," she said, putting the books down, puckering her brow, and pointing with one index finger to the "C" in "cat" and with the other index finger to the "C" in "cow," "are those the same because 'cat' starts out like 'cow'?"

At this rate she may teach herself to read before she enters nursery school.

5
Control for the Out-of-Control
A Child with Cerebral Palsy

CEREBRAL PALSY is a term now so widely used that I was surprised to learn it was coined as recently as 1930. Like many other medical terms it is not very apt. By palsy we usually mean shakiness or involuntary trembling in the elderly. But cerebral palsy is the term for a variety of disorders resulting from damage to the immature brain often occurring during the birth process, sometimes in the course of pregnancy, and sometimes in early infancy.

Typical victims of cerebral palsy who are able to walk are likely to shuffle and lurch from side to side. Their arms flop about jerkily. Their heads and shoulders may be twisted to one side. Often they cannot keep their mouths closed and thus cannot help drooling. If they try to speak, only those who have a lot of practice in listening can make out what they are saying.

Until about World War II, most parents of those so afflicted seemed to feel something like shame and tried to keep them hidden. This attitude can be traced all the way back to the authors of Leviticus, the third book of the Bible. It specifies who can and who cannot serve as a priest or priestly assistant and bars those who are "lame or broken-footed or broken-handed or crook-backed" (Lev. xxi, 18–20). Besides establishing that such unfortunates are somehow unclean, this lumps together all the crippled, making no distinctions among those who suffered brain injuries in infancy, those with genetic defects, and those afflicted later by diseases or accidents involving the nervous system, bones, muscles, or other parts of the body.

This confusion persisted until the middle of the nineteenth century. By then evidence that damage to the brain during infancy could cause lifelong physical crippling of the victim had been noticed by many students of medicine, but no one devoted much time to the subject. Such cases seemed hopeless.

It was a British surgeon, W. J. Little, who first demonstrated that not all such cases actually are hopeless. In 1843 Little delivered a series of lectures at London's Royal Orthopedic Hospital on his ways of working with them, those ways being basically the same as today's. He persisted in this work and in 1861 published a paper entitled "On the influence of abnormal parturition, difficult labor, premature birth, and asphyxia neonatorum, on the mental and physical condition of the child, especially in relation to deformities."

That paper was published in *The Lancet*, a British medical journal of great prestige and, although modern research has added a great deal to Little's findings, it has not fundamentally altered them. Yet for most of a century the paper and the rest of Little's work were ignored. Until the 1940s most victims of cerebral palsy continued to be hidden away or, in some cases, treated as comical village idiots.

No one seems to have tried to determine why it took so long for humane attitudes toward these agonizingly handicapped children to develop. It probably would take extensive sociological research into the attitudes of the public in general and the medical profession in particular. But at least they are no longer being kept out of sight and out of mind.

According to estimates by the U. S. Department of Health and Welfare the U.S. population now includes some 700,000 victims of cerebral palsy. That works out to about three of every thousand persons. Another estimate is that each year some 10,000 infants are born with this condition and more than 2,000 young children develop it as a result of injuries to their heads.

In plain language the chief cause of the precipitating brain damage is bad luck. Some cases can be blamed on misuse of forceps or anesthesia by an obstetrician or on some form of child abuse, but even these are likely to be temporary and unforseeable lapses by otherwise competent physicians or parents. Some are results of unnoticed and perhaps even undetectable accidents to the umbilical cord during pregnancy, temporarily cutting down the supply of oxygen to the fetus. Then there is precipitate labor, which can result in sudden, violent squeezing of the baby's head. On the other hand, prolonged labor exposes the baby to the possibility of many kinds of head injuries. In a few cases blood type incompatibility in the parents and infections of the mother during pregnancy or of the newborn infant seem to be to blame.

One reason why the explication of causes has to be vague is that cerebral palsy almost never is detected at birth. Only about two cases in five are discovered before the victim is six months old. Two out of three are noticed by the first birthday, but one in five goes undetected until after the child is three years old. Unless records of what went on during pregnancy and delivery are unusually detailed, such time lags make it very difficult to determine why and how the damage was done.

There are a variety of ways of classifying cerebral palsy symptoms, but most classifications are more complicated than useful. The two chief kinds of symptoms are the important ones. Three out of four victims are mostly spastic, meaning that the muscles affected are in more or less permanent spasm and can be relaxed voluntarily only with great difficulty, if at all. The others are mostly athetoid, meaning that the affected muscles make involuntary and uncontrolled movements. Those "mostlys" are mentioned because purely spastic or athetoid cases are rare, and a close observer usually can detect both kinds of symptoms. A very few of both types also have little or no sense of balance, the Latinate term for which condition is "ataxis."

The most rigid spastics, about one of every six cerebral palsy victims, are totally dependent on the help of others all their lives. At the opposite extreme, another one in six is so slightly handicapped as to be able to fade almost unnoticed into the general population. The other four out of six are distributed over the range between these extremes and may be affected only on one side.

"The most rigid spastics are totally dependent on the help of others all their lives."

That looks like a simple, straightforward sentence stating an unadorned fact. But it is the stuff of nightmares for anyone with even a moderately sensitive imagination. Cerebral palsy victims in general have only slightly shorter life expectancies than the rest of us. The most rigid spastics may live for several decades. What can it be like to live so long in speechless immobility?

To be sure, there is a high incidence of mental deficiency in those with severe brain damage, and such deficiency may leave the victims unaware of the horror of their situation. But a high incidence of mental deficiency does not mean that it is universal. It is possible that there are among the totally immobilized a few individuals with minds comparable to that of Christy Brown, a young Irishman just short of being totally immobilized by cerebral palsy. Unable to dress or feed himself, he had full use only of his left foot and wrote his autobiography, *My Left Foot*, typing one letter at a time with the little toe of that foot. He also wrote, the same way, a bestselling novel of the early 1970s entitled *Down All the Days*.

Although C. P., as I shall usually abbreviate it from now on, is not curable the way an infection or a broken limb may be, there is now a great deal that can be done to prevent such cases from getting so severely handicapped. This is no help to those already afflicted, of course. But in some cases what can be done now makes it seem mere hair-splitting to call C. P. incurable.

My best example is Chipper. He was a little over three months old when I first saw him. According to his mother, Sheila, her pediatrician had told her that "Chipper might have a little bit of cerebral palsy." This is like saying that a woman is a little bit pregnant, so I doubted that the doctor had phrased it quite that way. But it certainly was a mild case. It also was the earliest diagnosis I have encountered so far.

The first thing you noticed about Chipper was his liveliness. He was constantly squirming, reaching out, flailing his arms and legs, crowing, laughing, or, rather rarely, wailing. His two older sisters, aged three and five when I first started seeing him, seemed awed by him. When I called, they almost always were sitting in a corner playing as quiet as mice and talking to each other only in tiny voices.

"All we noticed about Chipper," Sheila told me, "was how active he was. When the pediatrician began to talk about a problem, I was scared that he was going to say Chipper was hyperactive and needed drugs. I really felt relieved when he mentioned C. P."

That could only mean she had no understanding of what it meant. And in the long run that lack of understanding may actually have been helpful. She stayed relaxed and probably was more useful to Chipper that way than if she had gotten scared and tense.

It took me several minutes of close observation to pick up the signs the doctor had noticed. Slim and wiry, with dark brown curls and gorgeous green eyes, Chipper was doing everything most three-month-olds do and usually doing it a little better than average. He raised his head and chest off the floor while lying prone and held that position for a minute at a time. When I picked him up, he brought his body together compactly and helped to maintain the position I held him in. He sat up with very little support and would even stand for a while if I supported him at the chest. And he showed great eye-hand coordination when I put a rattle in his hand.

And then I suddenly saw the pattern. He was favoring his right side, sometimes only slightly but now and then more pronouncedly. He kicked higher with his left leg. Often he kept his right hand fisted, but the left hand stayed open. The toes of his right foot often were curled under, and his right knee tended to stay extended.

All of which meant that he had excess tone in many of the muscles of his right side. Muscle tone is the degree of tension left in the muscles when they are at rest. Without such left-over tension we would collapse every time we relax. But its degree varies greatly from one person to another, even among those of us considered normal. At one end of the normal range are the wiry, tightly strung athletic or nervous types who have high muscle tone and usually look as if ready to leap into action. At the other end are the languid sorts of people who have low muscle tone and seem to melt into whatever pieces of furniture they come to rest on. Abnormally high tone is the cause of the spastic symptoms of C. P. victims, and uncontrolled variations from abnormally high to abnormally low tone are involved in athetoid symptoms. If the excess had been a little greater, the muscles would have gone into obvious spasm, and Chipper would have been obviously spastic. Whether they would ultimately have gone into obvious spasm if he had not been treated, no one will ever know—I am happy to be able to say.

It was clear to me right away that my job was going to be to help him make the effort to control the muscles of his right side. That meant slowing him down long enough to maintain positions in which he could feel the possibility of exerting more control there. I had, that is, to find ways to persuade him not to exercise in the usual sense of working harder and harder but in a way that would encourage him to support himself with his good left side while he tried to do a bit more with his not-so-good right side.

When I first phrased my problem like that to myself, it seemed it might be an extremely difficult one to solve. It struck me that Chipper's high level of activity was a sort of strategic wall he had built against having to make more use of his right side, that he kept going hard and fast in order to keep his mind off his weakness. But it took me only a moment to realize that this was much too fancy thinking. Chipper was so active simply because he was interested in everything around him and determined to express his interest. He used his right side as much as he could and would use it more as soon as he learned to trust it.

My best stratagem turned out to be a beachball about eighteen inches in diameter and not quite fully inflated. I put Chipper on it face down so that he sank into it a little. In order to raise his head and look around, which he usually and urgently wanted to do, he had to push up with both arms. If he did not push with equal force with both, he pushed himself off center and would start to slip sideways off the beachball.

To give him confidence I began by tipping the ball a little to his left so that he could do more of the work with his left side. Then, little by little, I tipped him more to his right. Working face to face with him, I could watch his reactions and increase the challenge to his right side to the most he could take, then quickly reduce the pressure when it got to be too much for him.

It's wonderful how much you can sometimes accomplish with a simple gimmick like this. Among other things, it was easy for Sheila to get the hang of it, so that she could work with him every day. We tried various other ways of making him use his right side more, of course, but in the end we always came back to the soft beachball. And by his first birthday the importance of my weekly visits was dwindling steadily.

Shortly after that anniversary he was walking with dashing confidence, and I pronounced him graduated from my care. It was impossible for me to detect any signs of abnormal muscle tone in his right side or of any tendency to favor that side in a way not usual in a left-hander. Since his father and father's father were left-handers, even his handedness was not unusual.

Yet Chipper's symptoms, though decidedly mild ones, were unmistakably the symptoms of C. P. and the results of irreversible brain damage. So what happened? The likeliest explanation, I think, is that the brain damage was so slight that other, undamaged parts of his brain were able to take over. His general alertness and quick reactions seem to add to the likelihood of this.

Whatever the explanation, he is one victim of brain damage who profited magnificently from early diagnosis and therapy. He may never realize that he suffered such damage. Even if he should, for instance, take up gymnastics and discover some day that he is able to do a one-hand stand on his left hand but not on his right, he probably will assume that this is because of his handedness. He may even be right.

But Chipper is an extreme case, by far the most lightly affected C. P. patient in my experience. More nearly typical was Jamie, one of a pair of much wanted and expected twins. They were wanted and expected because twins had become a tradition in their mother's family, and hand-me-down matching cribs, high chairs, a stroller, and other twin-babies' equipment were ready and waiting. Donna, their mother, had to start wearing maternity clothes after only a couple of months of pregnancy and scarcely needed the obstetrician's pronouncement that she was going to produce two offspring.

With a lot of huffing and puffing, she managed to waddle around until only a week before her due date. Labor started quietly and proceeded easily. The daughter, Janine, was born first, weighed about six pounds, and cried spontaneously. The son, Jamie, weighed only four-and-a-half pounds and had to be resuscitated. Although there was nothing greatly alarming about this, the hospital took the proper precaution of keeping him in an incubator for a couple of days, but it proved unnecessary to give him extra oxygen. The only other peculiarity noticed at the time was that Jamie took a bit longer than Janine to catch on to feeding.

He was eight months old when I first saw him. Looking back from that point Donna could not remember when she first began to suspect something wrong. She did remember talking to her pediatrician about things Janine was able to do that Jamie could not, but the doctor had been reassuring. No two children, he pointed out, ever develop at exactly the same rate; baby girls tend to develop a little more quickly than baby boys; and so on. Not until Jamie was almost eight months old did it become impossible to gloss over the differences between him and his sister.

There are some good reasons why many pediatricians are slow to recognize or, anyway, to point out to parents symptoms of C. P. in infants—reasons good from both the narrowly medical and the widely human points of view. I don't know why Chipper's doctor was an exception, but I suspect that one reason why Jamie's behaved more typically is that few physicians like to be bearers of bad news unless they can hope that news will do the hearer some good by making possible prevention or treatment. Obvious spasticity does not usually set in until a baby is over six months old, and many pediatricians still feel that there is not much point in therapy until the symptoms are obvious.

What makes this feeling possible is an unconscious assumption that is at last being challenged. That assumption flows from the incontrovertible, first-year-medical-school fact that, so far anyway, there is nothing that can be done to repair brain damage. Destroyed or damaged brain cells or other brain structures cannot yet be replaced or reconstituted. And this, of course, sets limits to what can be done for victims of such damage.

The question is: where are those limits? Those limits do not belong where it has been taken for granted they must be. There has been a highly effective challenge to the assumption that when brain damage causes abnormal muscle tone, as it does in C. P. patients, there is nothing that can be done about such muscle tone.

In my student days the "facts" about muscle tone were memorized and parroted back at exam time but had nothing to do with our treatment of such patients. About all we could do for any but the most lightly affected C. P. victims was a little stretching of shortened muscles, though we also sometimes were allowed to make not very hopeful attempts to persuade younger patients to try to get as close as possible to normal sitting, kneeling, standing, and other such positions. At best we were to be on the lookout for, and call to the attention of some pediatrician or orthopedist, evidence of overtightened tendons which a specialist might decide to release or lengthen by surgery.

When I went back to work as a physical therapist, I soon learned of a quite different approach to abnormal muscle tone. This had gotten underway in England in the 1940s. By the time I was in training in the late 1950s, news of its effectiveness was being published widely in highly respected British and European medical journals. Yet it was then, and still is, almost completely ignored by the American medical establishment.

So far as I have been able to determine, no villains have been involved in suppressing dissemination of the good news here. The problem seems to be merely that there is nothing substantial in it for any powers-that-be in American health business. No drugs are involved, so there is no reason for any pharmaceutical firm to turn loose high-powered press agentry. And since the basic discoveries are more than a quarter-century old, any American university or research center taking them up now risks being blamed for the long delay.

Berta and Karel Bobath were among the thousands of refugees from Central Europe who settled in Great Britain in the 1930s. She was a physical therapist and he a physician. In London she began specializing in work with children suffering C. P., and he later joined her in some of her work. Perhaps partly because she was an uprooted outsider, she soon found herself doubting and rethinking the usual approach to her patients.

This led her to seek clearer understanding of exactly how brain damage interferes with normal muscle tone. As is usually the case in original medical thinking, she got some of her insights through treating patients and some from the published papers of others who had worked in similar fields. Close to the heart of the matter, she found, was a single sentence in an obscure paper by a brain specialist who, himself, was quoting another research worker. Ms. Bobath quotes this quote in the introduction to one of her best books on her work with the forbidding title *Abnormal Postural Reflex Activity Caused by Brain Lesions* (Heinemann, London; 1965): "The cortex knows nothing of muscles, it knows only movements."

This may not look profound. Indeed, unless you are working in the field, it probably will take a while to figure out just what the sentence means. In essence, it states that the brain cortex does not operate the muscles individually—that is, it does not consciously contract, relax, or hold somewhere between these extremes any specific muscle. Rather, it seeks to bring about desired movements by orchestrating many muscle actions which are individually under control of lower nerve centers in the cerebellum, spinal cord, and elsewhere.

What makes the "not muscles but movements" observation profound is that the there's-not-much-we-can-do attitude toward C. P. patients is based, quite unconsciously, on the assumption that the brain *does* deal with muscles individually. This leads to the further assumption that the damage to the brain has, in effect, paralyzed the affected muscles. And that means there's-not-much-we-can-do.

Once Ms. Bobath had shed this assumption she was able to try to understand how brain damage actually does produce the symptoms of C. P. This led her to the study of the development of muscle coordination in infants who have not suffered brain damage. And this study led to her great discovery of the effectiveness of treating infant C. P. patients not as more or less hopelessly paralyzed but as victims of abnormal coordination of muscle action.

It was a two-pronged breakthrough. Besides giving us a new way of treating C. P. patients, it also has made possible early recognition of the symptoms. As already mentioned, many cases have gone undiagnosed through the first year or more of life. Now, even only moderately affected infants usually can be spotted in their early months by anyone who has trained in Ms. Bobath's methods.

The movements of newborn infants are a sort of random messing about. They may start as turns or lifts of the head or legs or whatever, and are likely to involve much of the rest of the body before they become fixed. Little by little, babies learn to coordinate such movements in order to get what they want. It takes practiced skill to perform even so simple-seeming an action as picking up a toy. Ms. Bobath's studies have established at approximately what ages normal infants develop the various skills and have broken many of the skills down into their component parts.

In Great Britain, Switzerland, and some other parts of Europe her methods have been adopted by the medical establishment and, reportedly, have greatly increased the rate of success in the treatment of young C. P. patients. In the U. S. it is only among physical therapists that they have become widely known. Eight-week training sessions for therapists, all centering on lengthy hands-on work with infant patients, are held several times a year in cities around the country. It is indicative of the enthusiasm generated by the success of trainees that I had to spend four years on a waiting list before my turn came around.

Training begins with detailed study of how infants develop, step by step, normal coordination of their muscle action. It makes an enormous difference to realize that what you are observing is mental effort, not to control specific muscles but to coordinate more or less automatic reflexes involving many muscles. *Mental* effort. That's the key. The baby knows what it wants to do and has to experiment with different combinations of movements—some automatic, some voluntary—in order to succeed.

Suppose, for instance, that a child is lying face down and chances to glimpse something it wants to get hold of and bring closer for a taste test. That involves several sets of reflex actions. Just to lift its head in order to get the eyes in position to focus on the object, it must coordinate the tensing and shortening of muscles of the back of the neck and shoulders with the relaxing and stretching of other muscles in the throat and chest. Other coordinations are involved in the actual focusing of the eyes, resting the weight on one arm, lifting and extending the other arm, grasping with the fingers, and so on.

We are not born knowing "instinctively" or any other way how to do all this coordinating. We have to learn to do it. And that learning process involves a great many trial-and-error experiments.

At first some of the experiments are bound to get the child nowhere—but only some of them and only at first in the course of normal development. If many of the experiments fail and the child persists in trying them again and again, getting in the habit of keeping some muscles abnormally tense, there probably has been damage of the parts of the cortex that should be involved in recognizing and dispensing with the failed experiments. A trained physical therapist can recognize the failures, inhibit a child from persisting in them, and make it easy and rewarding to try other, more hopeful experiments. If the brain damage has not been too severe and the child is not too set in bad habits, other parts of the brain may be able to take over some of the coordination of reflex activity.

But I'm not going to try to provide here a capsule course in the Bobath methods, which are formally known as Neuro-Developmental Treatment (NDT). Instead, I want to get back to Jamie and what I was able to do for him as a result of my NDT training. This is the best way to explain it in any case, because each patient is unique and has to be treated uniquely.

As I have mentioned, Jamie was eight months old when I began working with him. His mother, Donna, was still in something like shock at the time of my first visit. It was only a few days since the neurologist to whom her pediatrician had referred them had firmly placed the C. P. label on Jamie. Donna kept worrying about what it implied.

"Will he be able to walk? Some of them can't even talk or feed themselves. He can't be that bad, can he? Will he be able to ride a bike? Can he have children? Will he be mentally retarded? I don't know how to think about his future or anything. Is he going to die?"

She had known for some time that there was something wrong with Jamie, but the C. P. diagnosis had felt to her like a nightmare come true. No one could answer her questions with certainty, and that intensified her fears.

His very active twin, Janine, made things no easier for Donna. She had to keep Jamie in a small playpen.

"To protect him from her," she told me. "Janine is a hair puller and just crawls all over him. He can't defend himself at all. She doesn't mean any harm, but. . . ."

Donna started crying, I didn't try to stop her. I undressed Jamie and put him on his back on a blanket on the floor. He kicked a little, keeping his legs close together and turning the knees and toes inward. In normal kicking an infant separates its legs and turns the knees outward. When I pulled him up to a sitting position, he arched his back. When I put him face down, he made furious noises, tried to lift his head, could get it up only a couple of inches for a brief moment, and again wound up with his back rigidly arched.

He was obviously well on the way to becoming spastic. But when Donna finished her cry, I was able to show her that Jamie had a few strengths, too. He was quite alert visually and would follow with his eyes any moving object that interested him. He localized sounds, too, responding to his name by smiling and looking toward anyone who spoke it. I felt quite sure that he was not going to turn out to be severely retarded, if at all.

"Can you suggest something I can do with him?" she implored. "Some games or exercises? He must get awfully bored, lying there on his back all the time. But he seems miserable if I put him any other way."

This made me feel that I had come along at a good point and that she and I were going to be able to do Jamie some good. She knew little about C. P., but she had a feel for how things were with him. She would be willing to work hard to make even a little difference in his life. Such differences have to be very small at first, so her willingness was the indispensable ingredient.

In NDT terms, Jamie's arching of his back was a failed experiment. He had first tried doing it in an effort to orchestrate muscle reflexes and, although it didn't work, he was stuck with it. What Donna and I had to do was find ways to inhibit his persistence in that failure and motivate him to try new and different experiments.

Like many mothers of handicapped infants, she had grown unconsciously timid in the way she handled him. Even picking him up made her anxious because the way he went rigid made her feel that he was trying to pull away from her in pain or fear. So she had gotten in the habit of leaving him, as she had put it, "lying there on his back all the time."

This was decidedly not what he needed. Fortunately, I could see that there was a simple way of picking him up that would keep him from going rigid. All one had to do was turn him on his side and curl him into the fetal position before lifting him off the supporting surface. Instead of demonstrating this for Donna, I coached her to do it herself and wind up with Jamie on her hip, his legs parted, his arms around her neck, and her hands supporting him at his buttock and upper back. It worked beautifully. Jamie forgot about arching his back and started a few more experiments in head control made possible by this, for him, novel position. Donna, of course, was convinced that I must be some sort of genius.

The next step was to work out positions for him in which he could try new ways of moving all by himself. With this in mind I had brought along a wedge of foam rubber. After Donna had had a few minutes practice carrying him on her hip, I took him back from her and put him on the floor again, curling him into the fetal position in the process to give him the feel of a different kind of movement without his back arched. Then I put him face down on the foam wedge with his head and arms dangling over the high end.

If he had been a few months older, this might have been a very cruel thing to do to him. Once a spastic child has gone into full spasm, letting go can be terrifying. I have discussed this with adult spastics and other therapists, and most seem to agree that it is something like being stuck on a mountain ledge in the dark and forced to let go one's hold on the only means of support and step off with nothing but someone else's assurance that the step is safe.

But Jamie was still resilient enough not to panic. He whimpered a little, but when I dangled a toy in front of him, he not only stopped whimpering but actually tried an awkward swipe at it with both hands. For him this was a great try at a new kind of reflex coordination. I made sure Donna understood what he was doing and what a big step it was for him, then let him off the hook by picking him up and cuddling him in the fetal position again.

By then I was getting a good, clear feeling of how things stood with him. One of the most remarkable aspects of NDT training is that it gives a therapist the impression of being able, in effect, to link up with the nervous system of the baby being treated. For instance, Jamie had abnormally high muscle tone throughout his body, but I somehow already knew—without being able to say just how—that this was more so in his upper body than in the lower parts. More important, I "knew" that his habit of keeping many of his muscles either fully extended or fully flexed was not yet deeply settled and was going to be fairly easy for him to break in some cases.

At the end of that first session I spent a while keeping him curled in the fetal position while I rolled him slowly from side to side. Letting the rolling motion get slower and slower, I finally stopped it altogether with Jamie on his back. It was a good ten seconds before he went into the total extensions of his muscles usual for him in that position. That ten seconds of normal posture was an achievement for both of us.

In the weeks that followed I grew steadily more optimistic about Jamie. Donna and her husband, Jim, both were deeply committed to helping him and were quick to learn all I could teach them and to improvise on their own. Donna's mother was expert at designing and sewing things and made a great contribution in the form of a Jamie-size hammock which we hung in his playpen. This gave him a different way of lying on his back, curving his body so that his spine, shoulders, and legs were slightly flexed instead of fully extended. At first he could bear to be in it only a minute or so at a time, but Donna gradually extended his stays until he was spending several fifteen- to twenty-minute periods in it every day.

Getting him to try new ways of moving while lying on his front was the main objective for a while, and all of us worked on it. I encouraged them to check with me when they found something new just to make sure they didn't overdo it. One morning Donna called.

"Jim has a new one, and it seems to work great," she told me. "He lies on his back on the floor and puts Jamie face down on his chest. Then Jim makes funny noises. He barks and meows and quacks and mumbles and rumbles. Jamie loves it. He holds his head up and watches Jim's face with his eyes as big as saucers. And he keeps trying to imitate the noises Jim is making. Is it all okay?"

It was terrific, of course, and reminded me of the way Susie's mother had helped Susie get over the fear of lying prone. Besides helping Jamie enjoy the prone position and hold his head up, it was getting him to try meaningful sounds and requiring him to make many subtle little adjustments to Jim's breathing and other body movements. And it was making him a present of all that attention from his father.

These combined efforts soon produced great results. Jamie was able to hold his head up for a minute or more at a stretch. He went on to turning his head a little way to keep in view interesting things that moved past him, such as his romping sister. This way, he quickly discovered, he could follow her much farther than when he moved only his eyes, as previously.

Next we went to work on his abdominal muscles. These large, three-layered muscles are a sort of foundation for widely varied activities such as walking, manipulating objects with the hands, and even talking. In his months of lying extended on his back Jamie had made little use of them. When I first tried to get him to roll over, the only way he could make the effort was with his legs and back straight and stiff and his neck arched rigidly. In this position he would try to jerk himself to one side. It was an obviously doomed experiment in movement, making the abnormally high tone of many of his leg, trunk, and neck muscles even worse but using his abdominal muscles hardly at all.

Rolling over from back to front is a forerunner of walking, involving almost all the same muscles of the trunk, pelvis, head, arms, and legs. Normal babies practice it for months before going on to crawling, standing, and the first independent steps. If Jamie did not soon begin to get the feeling of using his abdominal muscles in rolling over, he would be delayed in learning to walk and might never be able to make much use of his hands or even to talk so that he could be understood.

So my task was to prevent him from continuing with his hopeless way of trying to turn over and get him to try new ways. What I wanted him to do was bend a little at the knees and hips and start over sideways with one leg, then follow through first with his trunk, then with his head, then with his other leg. And I wanted him to learn how to keep the whole process smooth, flowing, and relaxed, with none of his muscles either rigidly extended or tightly flexed.

I got down on all fours right over him, face to face. And as I tried to help him roll over, I could feel that for him the process just had to start with thrusting back his head and arching his neck. To short-circuit this, I kept one hand on the crown of his head and resisted his thrusting back that way. I kept my other hand on his abdominal muscles, alternately stroking and tapping to keep calling his attention to them. Donna sat beside his head, dangling and twitching a toy just below the edge of his vision to try to keep him interested in turning that way.

We made little progress in our first ten-minute session of this. But on my next visit a week later he was able after only a couple of minutes of it to let go enough so that I could turn him without having to fight his head thrust. So I taught Donna how to work this way with him and suggested that she try it two or three times a day, being careful not to tire him too much. After that he seemed to have progressed at least a step or two, and sometimes a lot, almost every time I visited. By a couple of months after his first birthday he could roll over in something very close to normal fashion and prop himself on his forearms with his neck only slightly arched.

One of the basic ideas of NDT is that, if you can help patients develop some normal movement, they will go on to develop more normal movement quite spontaneously. Jamie seemed to have read the book. His first big venture on his own was to roll over, prop himself on his forearms, then shift all his weight to one arm and reach out with the other to bat at a toy. Donna and I were so excited the first time we saw him do this that the noise we made frightened him almost to tears. Once we had soothed him, he got sort of cocky and tried to top his big scene by doing a primitive crawl movement, dragging himself forward a couple of inches on his arms.

As of this writing he is three months short of his second birthday, and we are still working out new approaches. We now have a gimmick we call a prone board, a heavily padded bit of plywood made by Jim. It can be propped up at one end so that when Jamie kneels on the lower end the upper one supports his chest. Wide straps around his back keep him from toppling off sideways and leave his arms free to play with toys. Or Donna can put him on the board on a kitchen counter top and let him watch her at her cooking or cleaning chores.

His grandfather is at work on a project of cutting down a standard tricycle to make a tiny one which will be an enormous help to Jamie in a few months if it works out. He'll probably need quite a while to learn to use it but, if he can, it will be great exercise for his legs and give him some very important independence. And the neighborhood troop of Girl Scouts have asked that, as soon as Jamie is up to it, they be allowed to take him and Janine to the nearby playground for an hour or so a couple of times a week.

All this help is going to make a tremendous difference for Jamie. He will always be recognizably spastic, with abnormally high muscle tone in some parts of his body. Anyone who wants to understand his speech probably always will have to make a real effort to do so, and it's likely he will need some kind of aid, perhaps a walker, to get around on his own. But I am almost certain he is going to find some way of moving about independently and perhaps even to live alone and take care of himself when he is an adult.

This is a very good prospect for a child as severely affected as Jamie. It took the combination of a fairly early diagnosis and help from a lot of people to make his future so hopeful.

Another patient of mine got no treatment until she was almost two and has had no really devoted help. Her prospects are heartbreaking.

A caseworker made the first appointment for me to see Clover. His directions were: "It's the house at the end of the third dirt road on the right after you pass the red corral." My only problem was in recognizing it when I got there. It was not a house but a decrepit shack. Up until then the term "rural slum" had not had much meaning for me. Since then, every time I have seen or heard it, that place has come back to mind.

Clover was twenty-two months old. Her family consisted of her three-year-old sister, Heather, and her twenty-four-year-old mother, Norene, who obviously long since had accepted utter defeat as her lot in life. She and her daughters had moved into the shanty a few weeks earlier from what probably was another one very much like it in a similar location a couple of hundred miles away. All three were intensely shy and sadly in need of baths.

Propped in the corner of a dusty overstuffed chair, Clover had a tangle of blond curls, bright blue eyes, a thick layer of grime, and obvious symptoms of severe cerebral palsy. Had she been getting any treatment where they used to live?

Norene: "No."

Had she ever been looked at by a doctor?

Norene: "No."

I had worked with the public health nurse in that area before and knew that she would really enjoy doing all she could for this unhappy family. I was able to reach her that afternoon and describe the situation. By the following week she had rigged up a washtub in front of the fireplace, the only source of heat, and had gotten the girls and their mother bathed, shampooed, and deloused and had succeeded in motivating Norene to remove some of the filth from the shack. She also had taken the girls to see a pediatrician and had arranged for them to get their immunizations at the health department.

The Head Start program accepted Heather, sent a bus to take her back and forth, and fed her two good meals a day. I had a feeling that other children her own age to play with and adults to talk to could make a big difference for her. The people who run the program work hard to get parents to participate, so there was even some prospect of drawing Norene out of her shell.

My work with Clover, however, produced no such hopeful results. One of her many symptoms was that when she went out of her most rigid, head-to-foot spasm, her head sagged to her right shoulder. Nothing I tried seemed to have the slightest effect on this pattern. I kept making suggestions to Norene about how to help Clover hold her head up, but I never saw any evidence that she did anything at all about it between my visits. For that matter, I'm not really sure she could have made much difference if she had.

I was able to promote for Clover a wheelchair with a special seat to give her support and a tray that fitted across the arms. Little toys on this tray gave her what probably was her first chance to try to manipulate anything. She got as far as pushing them off.

Because she had almost no communication with anyone, I racked my brains for something that would give her a chance to express at least a yes or no reaction. My best inspiration seemed to be two drawings of faces, one happily smiling and the other scowlingly unhappy. I pasted the happy one on the right side of her tray, the unhappy on the left side, and went to work to convince her that the happy one meant "yes" and the unhappy one "no." Eventually, she seemed to get the idea and sometimes would turn her eyes or slightly lean toward the appropriate side in response to questions such as: Do you want a drink? Are you ready to get in the car? Is that Heather's bus?

Whether I could ever have been of any real help to her I'll never know. One day I arrived for my weekly visit and found the shack abandoned, the front door hanging open and the family's few pathetic belongings gone, though the wheelchair still stood there. Later, the public health nurse told me she had learned from a neighbor that a male relative, possibly Norene's father or brother, had turned up in a pickup truck and had taken them away. I've never heard from or of them. All I can hope is that they are getting some kind of help somewhere.

It is possible that the future will be less bleak for infants as severely affected as Clover. There are rumors of drugs that show promise of lowering abnormally high muscle tone without producing dangerous side effects. Such a drug could provide the ideal starting point for neuro-developmental treatment. Cerebral palsy patients prevented from going into rigid spasm might be left weak, but this could make it easier to help them try new ways of putting their movements together.

6
Making the Most of It—Magnificently

A Child with Spina Bifida

Jenny was sitting at her desk reading and didn't notice when I turned up in the open doorway of her first-grade classroom. She is a beautiful child, blond, olive-skinned, and with her gleaming, shoulder-length hair tied back with a red ribbon. At first she seemed wholly absorbed in her book, but then I caught a sideways glance at the clock on the wall.

A bell rang. I backed out of the doorway to avoid damming up the rush to recess. When I could look inside again, Jenny was standing beside her desk with three other girls, one of whom was handing her crutches. Another of the three urgently announced, "I'll go guard our place," and ran past me.

"Come on, Jenny," said one of the two still with her. "You got four legs. You should be fastest."

Jenny laughed happily. Then she saw me.

"Hi, Kate. Did you come to see me?"

"Just wanted to say hello, Jenny. I saw your mom last week, and she told me you're in the Brownies and taking swimming lessons and doing your exercises every day. I figured I'd have trouble getting an appointment to see you, so I decided to come to your school."

"Aw, Kate," she said, grinning.

"You go play hopscotch now. We'll talk after recess."

Her teacher was delighted to have a chance to crow about Jenny's success as a first grader and even to listen to a little about my role in Jenny's life. It was four years since she had reached the age of three and graduated from working only

97

with her mother and me at home to a preschool for handicapped children. But Jenny has done so wonderfully well
against such overwhelming odds that everyone who has been
of any help to her will always have an interest in what and
how she is doing.

From the window her teacher and I could see the hopscotch
game. Jenny's legs are in braces, and she can walk, though a
little awkwardly, without further aid. She needs the crutches
only for maneuvers like running or hopping. At the game she
was playing she used just one crutch to help her keep balance
when she bent over to pick up the token. It was a great per-
formance for a child who had been born partially paralyzed
from the waist down.

Both on the playground and in the classroom, her teacher
told me, Jenny is one of her class's most popular members.
Her parents had wisely kept her in nursery school for an extra
year, so that she was six when she went to kindergarten and
seven on entering the first grade. She still is one of the smallest in her class but has a very helpful edge socially and intellectually. Physically, the only help she needs is in getting
in and out of the school bus, and she has made a game of that
by persuading the bus driver not to carry her down the steps
but to let her jump down them into his arms. He cooperates
by pretending to flinch away from her leg braces and tells
everyone that he is going to get the school district to buy him
a "Jenny-proof vest."

"She has a wonderful imagination," her teacher told me,
"and a nice sense of timing. When she reads aloud, the whole
class listens. I have a hunch she's going to wind up in some
kind of theatrical work."

Did Jenny have any trouble getting this acceptance at first?

None at all. The physical therapist currently working with
her had visited the classroom the day before Jenny first ap-
peared there. He took along braces and crutches for the other
children to try using and explained about how and why Jenny

had to use them. It proved the perfect way to break the ice for her.

"I once heard," the teacher told me, "a child new to the class say to Jenny 'I'm sorry you're crippled.' One of Jenny's friends spoke right up. 'She isn't crippled. She has spina bifida.' Jenny enjoyed the discussion. She smiled and said, 'That's right.' "

Spina bifida (prounounced SPY-nuh BIFF-id-uh) is Latin for "cleft spine," the use of Latin being justifiable in this case because the plain English could be taken to refer to a spinal injury occurring at any time of life. The Latin term designates a spinal cleft present at birth. The cleft is in one or the other of the vertebrae, the bone tissue of which fails to close around and thus provide protection for the nerves making up the spinal cord.

Surprisingly, minor defects in vertebrae are not at all uncommon. It has been estimated that at least one in ten and possibly as many as two out of three persons have an imperfect vertebra. For all but a tiny minority, to be sure, the imperfections are so slight that they cause no problems and go unnoticed throughout life.

The spina is considered to be bifida only if the vertebra is so badly formed that the spinal cord is exposed, or perhaps even protrudes, at birth, and this is the case with about three of every thousand infants born in this country. It usually means that the nerves involved have not developed normally. It also means that the meninges, the membranes enclosing the nerve tissue and spinal fluid, are exposed to infection. Until the development of antibiotics, such infection, called meningitis, meant almost certain death. Even now the best medical attention cannot save all the victims, and the necessary surgery does some inevitable damage to most of those saved in the course of returning the protruding nerve tissue to the spinal channel.

As is usually the case with spina bifida births, neither Jenny's mother, Sandy, nor her obstetrician had any hint of anything wrong before the baby emerged from the womb. But when the obstetrician saw the little balloon-like sac bulging from the spine low in the baby's back, he knew at once what it was and what it meant.

"It was an easy birth," Sandy told me later, "and Phil [her husband] was there with me through it all. We both saw that sac and realized that the doctor was upset by it, so we were, too. But about all we could get out of him in the way of information was the name spina bifida, the first time I'd ever heard those words. He told us they'd have to do some studies on the baby and that he'd have a specialist talk to us."

When the specialist showed up, he was sympathetic but full of frightening news. He gave them the background facts about spina bifida, warned about the great danger of meningitis, and then said that there was another, even more urgent, problem.

"Your baby's head is about half an inch more in circumference than it should be. Either she is producing too much cerebrospinal fluid, or the drainage system is not working properly. It's a problem that often turns up in spina bifida babies. It's called hydrocephalus, meaning brain water. Or, as laymen often say, water on the brain.

"That sounds terrifying, but the fact is that without a lot of fluid the brain would not function at all. In the fluid are dissolved, among other things, the sodium and potassium ions which pass back and forth through the membranes surrounding nerve fibers and, by doing so, maintain the strength of the electric impulses those fibers conduct. Each of us must produce in our brains, from materials supplied by the bloodstream, about three to five ounces of cerebrospinal fluid per day. Normally it flows around and through the brain to certain places where the bloodstream reabsorbs it. Blockage of the flow to those places causes buildup of excess fluid and pressure outward against the bones of the skull and inward on the brain tissue.

"Unless the fluid finds a way back into the bloodstream," Sandy's expert went on, "the damage it does to the brain will be severe, and the skull will be grotesquely enlarged. In the last few years we have developed a good procedure for installing a plastic tube to shunt excess fluid from the brain to a large blood vessel in the neck where it will be quite harmlessly absorbed. There is, though, always danger in any brain operation.

"As for the spinal lesion, we have a procedure for repairing it to some extent. And we have a good chance of being able to control infection of the meninges. But you need to know that your baby never will have fully normal functioning below the place of the cleft. That means not only leg functions but also bowel and bladder functions.

"You must also understand that, with all these problems, there is all too good a chance she simply will not have the strength to survive. Even though we are going to do for her absolutely everything anyone can do."

Sandy still remembers vividly every word spoken at that conference, which left her terrified but determined that her baby would pull through.

"Now," she recently told me, "I get the shivers whenever I go back over that time. Jenny is such a wonderful person, it still scares me to think she came so close to dying before she got a chance to live."

By the time I met Jenny, she was two months old and had proved quite as determined as her mother about surviving. The shunt had neatly solved the problem of excess cerebrospinal fluid, and the repaired cleft in her spine had healed over. However, in returning to the spinal channel the nerve tissue that had bulged out of it through the cleft, the surgeon had to remove some of the tissue, so the extent to which her lower body would be paralyzed still remained to be seen.

At that point Sandy had gotten all the comfort she could from her baby's success in surviving and was full of uncertainty about the future. It was a good time for me to come along. What she needed was a start on a program of what could be done to help Jenny make all possible use of her lower body. What's more, she knew that was what she needed, so I had to do nothing about convincing her.

The first thing that struck me about Jenny was the way she smiled at her mother. It seemed to me—or perhaps I should say that I had a sort of fantasy—that she was trying to reassure Sandy. Although it had no effect on Sandy, because she was too tense to really respond to it even when I insisted on her noticing, it made me feel quite hopeful.

I suppose I was grasping at the one available straw. What I had been told about this baby was very gloomy. From all the medical reports, she had only minimum sensation below where her spine had been damaged.

"One of the loveliest smiles I've ever seen," I persisted.

"Well, I'd rather have her frown," said Sandy, "if it would mean she could use her legs. Sometimes I feel I'll go crazy thinking about her in a wheelchair all her life."

"It seems like a terribly limited life to us but I know several people who have spent their lives in wheelchairs and do everything but walk. But we can't be anything like sure she's not going to walk. It's up to us—you and me—to give her all the motivation and stimulation she can handle to make all possible use of her legs. It'll probably be years before she reaches her limits if we help her keep working toward them."

This, of course, is good common as well as medical sense. Left strictly to her own devices any infant with little sensation in her legs and full sensation in her arms and trunk would tend to neglect her legs. By frequently calling Jenny's attention to her legs, we could gradually make her more aware of them. That would lead to her taking more notice of what sensations she does get from her legs and making more effort to order them to do things.

Before we could profitably go to work on Jenny's legs, though, it was necessary to get her as interested as possible in voluntary movement generally. Her long stay in the hospital and immobilization during the healing of her surgical wounds had held her back from the usual infant experimentation with random movements. Also, it was going to take quite a while to get results with her legs, if any were possible. Sandy needed to see that the kind of work I was proposing—only an hour or so a week of it for me but many hours every day for her—could really be effective.

I decided to start with rolling from side to side, which I knew Jenny soon would be trying on her own. Putting her naked on her back in the middle of a small blanket on the floor, I stationed Sandy with a squeaky and bright red doll on Jenny's right. Sandy held the doll at floor level and squeaked it. As Jenny turned her head to see, I gently lifted the left edge of the blanket and rolled her slowly a little way toward her right side. When I lowered the blanket, she rolled onto her back.

For the first couple of weeks we stuck with this and a few other little exercises to help her coordinate vision and trunk movement, and I showed Sandy how to stimulate her skin by rubbing with cloths and brushes of different textures. By my third visit Jenny was enthusiastically going all the way over onto her stomach. What was more, in the process she was making a few very slight but unmistakable movements with her legs. Sandy hadn't noticed and got quite excited when I called her attention to these. I was a little concerned about raising her hopes too high, but I had a hunch that we could forget about that wheelchair.

At my suggestion Sandy also put Jenny in an infant seat for brief periods several times a day. The idea was to give her practice in holding up her head and trunk. Watching her at this I again caught a few little movements of her legs. It may have been some sort of automatic attempt to help her maintain her balance.

That convinced me we could go to work directly on her awareness of her legs. Besides skin stimulation, there are many ways to do this. One is to gently push and pull at the hip, knee, and ankle joints. These points are liberally supplied with proprioceptors (receptors of one's own inner sensations) which keep firing off nerve impulses and thus keep us aware quite literally of where and how we stand. Jenny's proprioceptors were all right, but many of the connections to her brain via her spinal column had to be cut away during the surgical repair of her spinal cleft.

To help me get the hang of how things must feel to her and other patients like her, I like to imagine that theirs are something like the sensations I get when one of my feet or legs goes to sleep. This involves temporary suppression of some of the flow of nerve impulses from proprioceptors. To me the sensations that do get through seem dull, vague, uninteresting, not quite believable as really my own.

An adult outpatient I worked with in my student days helped me understand about this. A stroke had paralyzed his left side, and his wife brought him in three times a week for help in regaining use of his muscles. When he at last began getting a few vague sensations from his proprioceptors on that side, he told me at one session:

"I know that's my left leg. I see it and recognize it. But it just doesn't feel like mine or behave like mine. If I could, I'd rather ignore it. I'm not here because I want to feel it but because I know I've got to if I'm going to be able to take care of myself again."

Jenny had never had a chance to get acquainted with her legs, so she didn't really know them as hers and had no idea of how important they could be to her once she got in touch with them. Besides stroking the skin and putting various kinds of pressure on the joints, we tried a lot of other ways of attracting her attention to them. We kept our eyes open for vividly colored and patterned booties and soon had a collection of stripes, checks, polka dots, and calicoes in bright reds, oranges, blues, yellows, greens, and purples. To some of them we sewed devices that squeaked or squawked or tinkled or rattled when pressed or moved. And whenever it was time for Jenny to lie down, Sandy would slip a pair of booties on her feet and wave the feet about to attract her attention to them or prop them up with a pillow to keep them in her line of sight.

She was fascinated, of course, and kept reaching out toward them with her hands. Every once in a while, Sandy would gently bend one of Jenny's legs so that she could get hold of the foot. She would hold and examine it with great concentration. When she let go, it would slowly and apparently automatically return to its natural position.

For several weeks this was all that happened. Then one day after working with her on leg stimulation for a while, Sandy and I were sitting at the table and chatting over cups of tea. Jenny lay on her back on a blanket on the floor, her feet clad in crimson and white booties and propped on a cushion. Sandy was saying something about feeling a little down because of lack of progress when I chanced to glance at Jenny. She was holding her left foot close to her face with both hands and giving the bootie a thorough examination.

My little shriek startled her, and she let go the foot. I smiled at her and spoke reassuringly, keeping Sandy with me at the table. Soon Jenny's interest returned to her foot. While we watched breathlessly, she extended her hands as far as she could reach toward it, slowly lifted it to meet them, then pulled it toward her face. It was one of those great moments that make weeks and weeks of effort worthwhile.

We had to make do with it for quite a while so far as her legs were concerned. Until she was about seven months old this was the only kind of voluntary leg movement we ever saw her make. But any such movement was infinitely better than none.

She made rapid progress, however, in all infant skills involving her head, shoulders, arms, and trunk. Sometimes she even seemed a bit precocious, considering how much of her first two months she had spent immobilized. She did very well at movements like lifting her head while lying on her stomach and, later, lifting and supporting her trunk with her arms or holding her head steady while being pulled to a sitting position.

With help and encouragement her rolling from her back onto her stomach, as I have described, soon led to stomach-to-back rolls and then to rolls on up to a sitting position. She was quick at the commando crawl, too, though she used only her elbows for propulsion and merely dragged her legs along. Because I could find no successful way to get her to try digging in with her knees, we skipped that stage and tried to prepare her for the quadruped, hands-and-knees position.

This was a big test. I felt sure that if she could crawl on her hands and knees she would eventually be able to walk. Quite on her own, she already had taken to raising her head and trunk and supporting the weight with her hands and arms. One day I caught her at this, gently raised her rear end, too, and arranged her legs so that she could support its weight on her knees.

Though Sandy and I stroked her and murmured reassurance, Jenny whimpered a little. To help her feel more secure I made a sling out of a big, soft towel and put it around her middle so that Sandy or I could help her hold up the weight of the lower part of her body. But this was supposed to be only a temporary and mostly psychological aid. Even a paraplegic can hold the all-fours position if someone helps place the knees in proper position under the hips so that the bones carry the weight and need no help from muscles.

Jenny's whimpers were only from natural fears about trying something new. That very first time we had her up on all fours I could feel that she was flexing, ever so slightly, some of the muscles in her hips and thighs. At that stage, of course, the flexing could not possibly be anything but slight. Muscles have to be used in order to develop any strength, and she had as yet made scarcely any use of those in the lower part of her body.

Although I knew it was far-fetched, I had a vision of her as an explorer newly landed on the shore of an unknown continent. It was a useful metaphor because it took her a long time to get the hang of the new territory and start probing it here and there. For weeks she could do no more than hold the position, and she whimpered if we tried to remove the supporting sling. But eventually her hip muscles grew strong enough so that she could hold steady without the sling and even move her head around to look at toys or other attractions which Sandy or I held or shook or squeaked at various points just out of her range of vision.

Next, we reinstated the sling so that we could rock her back and forth and from side to side. This involved new muscles and new balancing problems, so again weeks of practice with the sling were necessary before she could do without the sling. A few more weeks went into persuading her to support her weight on her knees and one hand while she reached out to pick up a toy with the other hand.

By the time she was able to do all this without the sling, her leg and buttock muscles were noticeably larger, and I decided it was time to try to get her to crawl. The day I announced this to Sandy we got Jenny onto her hands and knees, made sure she was happy that way, then dropped to our own hands and knees and crawled around the floor talking, laughing, and calling to her. I still think it was a good idea and might be a big success with some infants in the right stage of development and the right mood. Jenny was not in the mood. She stayed stock still and stared at us with the look of a dowager forced to witness a faux pas until we both collapsed in laughter at her expression and our own feelings of foolishness.

So we went back to the towel sling. While I held it, Sandy got down on her hands and knees beside Jenny and demonstrated slow crawling, moving first her right hand, then her left knee, then her left hand, and finally her right knee. After the demonstration Sandy came back alongside Jenny and started the process over again while I gently pulled Jenny forward with the sling.

I suspect that Jenny's reaction had about it more than a touch of self-assertive contrariness. I was not only pulling her forward but also pulling more on her right side so that she would move her right side first. My intention was to shift the pressure as soon as she did so in an effort to get her to move her left leg next. First, she resisted doing any moving at all for as long as she could hold out, then suddenly hopped forward rabbit-fashion, first with both arms and then with both knees. She did it so quickly that I lost my balance and fell to one hand.

Sandy was alarmed, but I was able to assure her that a sizable minority of infants with no handicaps do their first all-fours moving in little hops of this sort. Jenny's choice of that way was no indication of any neurological problem. She kept on doing it that way whenever we put the sling around her and tried to urge her forward. At first we held her to only three or four hops at a time, but over the next few weeks Sandy gradually extended sling time until Jenny was hopping all around the room and needing less and less support from the sling.

She seemed afraid to try without the sling, or perhaps it was just that her legs were too weak. There was no need to hurry her, though. We kept on putting her through many other kinds of workouts, some with steadily improving results. The side-to-side rolling, for instance, soon progressed to the point where she could go all the way from flat on her back to up on her hands and knees with no help at all.

Then one day came the kind of phone call I've learned to expect sooner or later from others like Sandy.

"We were doing some stretching exercises," she told me in great excitement. "I got thirsty, so I left her on her back on the blanket on the living room floor and went to the kitchen for a glass of water. When I came back, there she was, crawl-

ing all by herself. Perfect technique. Right hand then left knee
then left hand then right knee. All around the room. She's
been at it for several minutes and still going strong. What a
day!"

By then Jenny was a little over a year old. She laughed
and babbled a lot, said "mama" and "dada" and "baybay"
and a few other syllables, and sometimes would try to repeat
something she heard. She fed herself finger foods and waved
byebye. Lying on her back, she often waved her legs around
quite vigorously in ways much like the practice kicking that
six-month-old babies with intact spines go in for.

Sandy and Phil had gained confidence in their ability to
give her the help she needed and were growing more and more
hopeful about the long run. The specialists they checked with
from time to time remained guarded in their assessments of
Jenny's potentials. Finally, Sandy had heard "let's wait and
see" one time too many. She made an appointment for her
and Phil to take Jenny for evaluation at a spina bifida clinic
in a nearby city.

A team including a neurologist, orthopedist, pediatrician,
physical therapist, psychologist, social worker, speech therapist, urologist, ophthalmologist, and surgeon spent two days
studying Jenny. Her parents did their waiting in the company
of several other parents of spina bifida children of a variety
of ages, life styles, and degrees of handicap. Phil came back
enthusiastic about the whole experience, and Sandy agreed
with him in his presence. But when we were alone together,
she told it differently.

"I've been concentrating so hard on her progress—I've been
so excited about it that I had sort of forgotten where we
started from. Sitting in that waiting room with all of those
other families, it really hit me. I have a defective child. She
has a defective spine and a defective lower body, and they're
always going to be that way. Defective. It's a repulsive word.
But she's my baby and I'm going to do absolutely everything
I have to do to see that she gets all the help she needs and

can use. I'm going to make that word 'defective' mean less and less."

Jenny's evaluators said that she was functioning at her age level in personal and social skills, in pre-verbal skills and in hand-eye coordination tasks such as putting blocks in a box and squeezing a toy to make it squeak. In everything involving her lower body she was, obviously, a good deal delayed. In alertness and ability to learn, by which they meant intelligence, they judged her to be at the upper normal level. Her "sensory deficit," meaning the loss of sensation resulting from the damage to her spine, they judged only to be considerable but not yet to be determined with anything like finality.

None of this really was news to Sandy and Phil, but they were glad to have it made explicit, especially the part about Jenny's intelligence.

"The hydrocephalus business scared me," Sandy said. "Or anyway, the doctors scared me when they talked to us about it the day after she was born. I registered 'brain damage,' and I've been sort of holding my breath about it ever since. At some level I've known for a long time that she's as bright and alert as I could hope, but somehow I needed to have those people make it official."

Sandy did not seem to notice that the question about the amount of sensation Jenny might eventually have in her lower body involved more than whether she would be able to walk. It also involved bladder and bowel control. There would be no question of toilet training for many months yet, however, so I decided on a policy of wait and see.

By the age of fifteen months Jenny was crawling all over the house and doing a great deal of kicking while lying on her back or stomach. This is the way babies acquaint themselves with and then gradually strengthen their leg muscles in preparation for standing and walking. Jenny was months behind ordinary children in this, of course, so we did all we could to encourage her to kick out.

One stratagem was to tie bells and bracelets around her

ankles so that the kicking would produce noise and bright flashes of light. Another was to lay her prone on the kitchen counter with her legs in the sink full of warm water. She delighted in transferring most of the water to the floor.

As usual, she soon rewarded us. One morning she was crawling around the living room floor while Sandy and I watched. I was just commenting on how nicely her behind was filling out when she approached the couch, reached up to grab a cushion first with one hand, then with both, and slowly pulled herself to standing. She held that position for half a minute or more and smiled knowingly in acknowledgment of our praise.

When we got her back down and she resumed crawling, Sandy went to the kitchen and fetched two glasses and a bottle of wine.

"We've just got to drink to that," she crowed. "I know you've felt all along that she was going to walk, and you've given me faith, too. But now I guess I really believe it some way I couldn't before."

I joined her in the toast to Jenny. She had a long way to go yet before she would be walking, but she certainly had come a lot further than she still had to go.

In the next few days Jenny began pulling up to standing alongside anything and anyone she could get a purchase on. She was about seventeen months old, eight or nine months older than the usual age for first standing, but that did not take away from her triumph. She was doing it with fewer than half the neural pathways most of us are equipped with in our legs and lower backs.

Her feet twisted under her, though, and her toes also rolled under tightly when she stood. So it was clear, as we had expected, that she needed braces to help her keep everything properly aligned in the standing position. An orthopedist prescribed lightweight plastic supports.

It took Jenny three days to determine for herself that the braces were not instruments of torture but sources of help.

They did not actually hurt her, of course, but they did cost her much of the great flexibility of her feet. Because of her limited sensation from them and limited control over them, she had been using them like a pair of Raggedy Ann dolls. That was all right for crawling but not for standing and walking. In three days, though, Jenny stopped missing the flexibility and began making use of the new stability.

Her first movements while standing in her braces were sideways along the living room couch. Leaning against it with her chest and reaching out with her hands for toys and other interesting objects I had strewn along it, she happily sidled up and down for ten minutes and seemed willing to go on for much longer. I had to call a halt because I was afraid she might tire her feet and legs more than the few sensations getting through from them would permit her to realize.

This sidling movement along some sort of support, such as a couch, is for almost all children the first kind of walking, and the reason why is interesting. For us bipeds it takes a lot of skill to maintain balance while walking and a lot of strength in many different sets of muscles. We give most of these muscles preliminary use and strengthening in the course of our infant kicking, crawling, and such. But we do not, before standing erect, make much use of the specific buttock muscles that move the legs sideways. Since occasional small sideways movements are essential to the delicate task of maintaining balance, we begin our walking with sidling in order to strengthen these muscles.

After a couple of weeks of sidling, Jenny had built up enough strength to cruise around holding someone's hand, still going mostly sideways but now and then trying experimental steps forward. I borrowed a tiny walker with wheels for her that could be braked so that they wouldn't roll too fast. By her twentieth month she was getting around confidently forward and backward so long as she had the walker or some other support to hold onto.

At this point we chanced on a little demonstration of the strangeness of the way she experienced the world with the lower part of her body. When I arrived at her home one afternoon, she was in her walker and scooted at her top speed across the living room to greet me. Apparently, one wheel of the walker ran across a pencil lying on the floor and lifted it at just the time and angle for her to kick against the point with the side of one bare foot. Jenny gave no indication of noticing the wound at all and took little interest even in her mother's cleaning of it while I held her. A few moments later she was sitting on my lap deeply absorbed in a bead-stringing test I had brought for her. Suddenly, she broke out of her absorption to look with a frown at her scratched foot. A piece of soft tissue paper in which the test had been wrapped was brushing against the skin on the side opposite the scratch. She reached down and pushed it away.

Every once in a while I try to imagine what it would be like not to register a bad scratch but to feel clearly a soft, light, brushing touch. I can't say that I've had any success. But since then Sandy has made it a point to be sure Jenny wears shoes, or, at least, good thick socks whenever she is on her feet.

Shortly before her second birthday I took her a pair of tiny crutches. She found them great but not for the purpose intended. She was just launching into the Terrible Two period, the time of first asserting independence, saying an emphatic NO to almost every suggestion and trying an occasional bit of aggression. At that point her only possible use for a crutch was as a club. Anyone within crutch reach who failed to please her—and often there wasn't any way to please her—could expect to be whacked at.

More successful from our point of view was a set of parallel bars her father built for her. She started by using only one bar at a time and sidling along it. We carefully avoided any indication that this was not exactly what we wanted her to do. She soon switched to hopping along between the bars with one hand on each. Again, we avoided either approving or disapproving, and within a week she tried and found that she preferred a one-foot-at-a-time gait.

Sandy and I managed to interest her in a few other exercises by using music to get around her contrariness. Paying no visible attention to her, we would put on a record, lie on the floor, and do leg lifts in various positions and more or less in time with the music. Or we would stand on one foot and hop about. Then came a Saturday morning swim class for handicapped children at a local pool where high school and college student volunteers worked with the children in the water one-on-one. Jenny took right to it.

Her first braces had been made with a fixed ankle so that her foot was held firmly at an angle of 90° in relation to her leg. Soon after she passed the two-and-a-half mark, her orthopedist prescribed new braces with little springs at the ankles making possible a variation of about 5° in the foot angle. These allowed her to walk in the usual heel-to-toe fashion—that is, by coming down on her heel and rolling forward to her toe.

Once she was able to walk easily between the parallel bars with the new braces, she was ready for more conventional use of the crutches, and she learned how to use them almost without help. The last few months before she reached three and graduated from my care went into practice in walking with the crutches over rougher and rougher terrain, climbing shallow stairs and getting back up when she fell down. She did it by first settling herself in a sitting position, doing a little counter twist of her trunk to the left, then twisting hard back to the right and on up onto her hands and feet. She pushes the last bit of the way up with her crutches. With braces on this is a difficult maneuver, but Jenny makes it look easy.

That was the last thing I helped her with. Since then my involvement in her life has been merely as one of her fans. Sandy and the therapists and teachers in Jenny's schools have kept me posted.

One of her triumphs has been as big sister to the second daughter Sandy produced when Jenny was just past three. There is increased risk of spina bifida in a family that has had one child afflicted with it, but Sandy's obstetrician assured her that amniocentesis would determine in the first couple of months of pregnancy whether the fetus had any spinal cord problems, so she and Phil decided to try again. The second baby, Diana, had no sign of spine trouble and quickly became the light of Jenny's life, far more interesting to her than her dolls.

"She feeds Diana," Sandy told me, "and reads to her and plays with her by the hour. Some days she takes over so many of my chores that I get to feeling a little guilty."

By her fourth birthday Jenny had learned to walk around indoors, where the footing is dependably even, without crutches. In the following year she learned to run outdoors with the help of crutches, using them mostly as reserve extra legs for when she has any balancing difficulties. They seem to give her confidence, and she has little trouble keeping up with her playmates. In some activities such as maze crawling, sliding, and swinging she seems expert, and she has long since graduated from a tricycle to a small bicycle.

She still has in her brain the shunt placed there to help drain excess cerebrospinal fluid. It probably is no longer necessary to her but it does no harm, and the operation to remove it might do some. She probably will keep it for life and forget its existence.

Her bowel and bladder problems have been solved, the bowel one quite easily. She can have a bowel movement only with the help of a suppository, and one of these every other day is all that's necessary. But chafing from constantly dribbling urine and a couple of bladder infections as a result of occasional pooling of urine finally led a urologist to advise an operation. Performed the summer before she entered first grade, this drains the urine through a tiny hole in her side into a little bag that she can easily remove, empty, and replace. The result is that she now does consciously with her hands what most of the rest of us do more or less subconsciously with our bladder and rectal muscles.

Her orthopedist thinks that, when she is nine or ten, he will be able to stabilize her feet surgically so that she can do without braces. Strangers encountering her after that may notice that her walking gait is a little stiff. Or they may not. It certainly will astonish them to learn that she is partially paralyzed from the waist down.

With her intimates, of course, it will be another matter. Her social life and sex life certainly are going to be affected by her handicaps and stratagems for overcoming them. But no part of her life is going to be determined by her handicaps.

"Jenny," her father recently said to me, "isn't and never will be a sweet, docile person. She can be a real spitfire. Sometimes I think she's got too much spunk. We've had to pull on her reins some already, and I shudder to think what it's going to be like when she reaches her teens."

It is easy to understand why a parent of such a child would worry a bit. But it is precisely because Jenny is that kind of a person that she is able not just to live with her handicaps but to live with them triumphantly.

7
When Nothing Can Be Done
Three Infants Beyond Help—and Hope

It USUALLY is possible to do a great deal for infants born with handicaps. For about one of every ten children I am asked to work with, however, there is nothing that physical therapy, surgery, or any other kind of treatment known today can do. To keep this account in balance I am going to report in this chapter on three such cases.

Both Marlene and her husband, Joe, had several brothers and sisters plus cousins, aunts, and uncles. As the time for the birth of their first child drew near, their large families generated a lot of enthusiasm and engulfed them with heirlooms, including a crib more than a century old. They planned on a natural birthing with Joe present to coach her, but after prolonged labor the obstetrician decided that the baby was showing signs of distress. He decided a Caesarean was necessary to save its life.

"It's a boy," he told Marlene when she came out of anesthesia. "He's big, well-formed, dark-haired. But there are some problems. Breathing trouble. Seizures. I'm afraid there's been an insult to the brain."

Marlene told me she almost laughed. The idea of someone insulting her baby's brain struck her as funny. But that feeling did not last when she learned that an "insult" meant damage to the brain.

The doctor went on to explain that the umbilical cord had started deteriorating at least several hours and perhaps a day or two before the baby was born. The insult was the resultant

117

cut-off of the supply of oxygen to the brain during that period. Joe and the baby and a nurse were on their way by plane to an intensive care unit at a city two hundred miles away.

"Will my baby be all right?" she asked.

"It's too soon to say, but he'll get the best care possible."

Marlene suddenly realized that they had not even named the baby. She cried off and on for hours.

By the time I first saw Jonathan, as he finally was named, he was almost three months old, and it had been established that only the lower, more primitive parts of his brain were functioning. No explanation had been found for why his umbilical cord deteriorated. Its failure left him, in effect, mindless and subject to frequent convulsions. The medication he had to be given to dampen the effect of the spasms kept him limp.

The pediatrician told me that anything I could do to improve the child's poor muscle tone, however slightly, would be a plus. He did have a sucking reflex. Since sucking involves the neck flexors, the muscles that pull the head forward and downward into a tuck position, I tried offering him a pacifier to suck while I held him in a semi-sitting position, the idea being to get him to try controlling his head movement. Occasionally, I would get the feeling that he was making a small effort, but the feeling soon evaporated.

Neither Marlene nor I gave up easily. We tried all kinds of movements holding him in our arms and bouncing around the room, swaying, dancing, and so on. A few times we felt rewarded by seeing him open his eyes and seem to gaze at something. But he always closed them again within a few seconds.

Once when I was holding him he lifted his head, and I felt a wave of tension sweep over his body. I got excited. Marlene let me down as gently as she could.

"I'm afraid," she said quietly, "that it was a seizure."

At eight months he seemed the same as at three months. All he could do was eat and sleep. So one of our social workers broached to his parents the subject of placing Jonathan in an institution.

The chief point of this book is that we have come a long way since such placing was the usual fate of children greatly delayed in their development and for whom it meant the end of hope. But Jonathan was not merely delayed in development. No matter how often or how artfully we offered him stimulation and encouragement, they could do him no good. He could not notice what we were doing. We never had any evidence that he noticed us.

Even before the social worker—I'll call him Jerry—brought up the possibility, Marlene and Joe had talked about seeking a place for Jonathan. Inevitably, they felt guilty. But they wanted other children, there being no indication of anything genetically wrong with Jonathan, and his utter helplessness meant that caring for him at home would leave Marlene little time for any others. So when Jerry made his suggestions and I responded to Marlene's questions by agreeing that it seemed to me a sensible solution of their problem, they decided to visit the place Jerry named, found it remarkably pleasant, and agreed to take Jonathan there.

It is in a small town about three hours from us, and on the appointed day Jerry arranged to drive the three of them there. The night before the trip he had a nightmare. In it the child wailed in despair and accused him of being in criminal league against it and of consigning it to a fate worse than death.

I mention this in defense of social workers generally. Several recent books, films, and television programs have pictured them as bureaucratic persecutors of the urban poor who sadistically enjoy their power to cut off welfare payments. Almost all those I have known sympathize so strongly with their clients that, like Jerry, they tie themselves in emotional knots trying to solve the frequently insoluble problems they deal with.

In this case the knot undid itself. When the four of them

arrived, they found that the ward to which Jonathan was assigned was a small, pleasant room with cribs for a dozen babies in care of a nurse. She knew her job well, liked it, and treated her helpless and hopeless charges with respect. A physician would see each child at least once a day, and specialists were on call in cases of emergency.

"It was obviously the perfect place for Jonathan," Jerry told me. "They give him all the attention for which he has any conceivable use."

Marlene and Joe visit him there whenever they feel like it and bring him home for a few days at Christmas or on his birthday or whenever they want to have him with them.

So—the ideal solution had been found? Unfortunately, not quite.

Joe has a small business of his own and a health insurance policy which he understood covered the birth of his son. It turned out that the fine print specified no coverage for anything extraordinary that might develop during the baby's first month of life. The cost of the care Jonathan received during that period was more than $20,000, which Joe had to scrape up by taking out a second mortgage and by borrowing from family and friends. And now the cost to taxpayers of keeping Jonathan where he is comes to a couple of thousand dollars a month while all goes well—much more when he develops symptoms requiring intensive care, which he is bound to do from time to time.

All this expense raises a harrowing question. It seems only reasonable that some public agency should provide help with such a child. But when a public agency does take the baby, is there a point at which a halt should be called in the expenditure of public money? In other words, is it reasonable to spend so much on hopeless cases?

I do not have the answer. About all I can offer in the way of response is the hope, which I doubtless share with most other human beings, that I never am the one forced to decide to call a halt.

Only a very few children are so severely handicapped that the kind of custodial care provided Jonathan is all they need. I have had only two other patients for whom I was able to do so little. In Jonathan's case it soon became clear that I could not do much, if anything. In Becky's case I kept hoping and hoping.

She was five months old when I first saw her. It was a public health nurse who got me involved. Becky's father was a short order cook and her mother a motel chambermaid. They had no health insurance and seemed unable to follow suggestions about how to seek help.

At first encounter Becky would have seemed to me merely an unusually plump and placid baby if the public health nurse had not filled me in. The problem was that she was very much too placid. She lay completely inert for hours at a stretch. Even her eyelids seldom flickered.

Her mother also was a good deal overweight and quite shy. She asked me no questions at all, but she seemed fond of Becky and interested in my demonstrations of how to stimulate various parts of her body and how to hold her to encourage her to use her own muscles. She also seemed willing to accept my suggestions about not leaving the baby alone in bed all the time but keeping her as much as possible wherever the action was in the house.

Eventually, Becky saw a pediatrician at a local clinic. He set up an examination by a neurologist and arranged for a chromosome study. In both cases the results were negative. All agreed that Becky was overweight and remarkably inactive but could find no genetic, neurological, or other such abnormalities. The pediatrician suggested only that I continue working with her.

"I can see no reason," he said, "why there should not eventually be some improvement, perhaps even enormous improvement."

So I kept on spending an hour or so with her and her mother every week, trying everything in my repertoire. We swung Becky, bounced her, rubbed and stroked her, tempted her with brightly colored toys and toys that made interesting noises and lights that flashed and flickered. Her only reactions were a few remarkably ambiguous sounds; they may have been protests but could have been expressions of pleasure.

Because her mother also was overweight, we were afraid she might be overfeeding Becky, but the public health nurse kept checking up and finally was sure that this was not the trouble. The baby was so fat simply because of her inertness. It also was at least partly responsible for her low resistance to colds and other ailments. It takes normal activity to develop muscle tone, promote good circulation, and maintain general good health.

When Becky was about ten months old, one of her colds developed into pneumonia, and it took hospitalization to save her. She had been home only a couple of weeks when she caught another cold. This one did not seem so bad at first, but it worsened suddenly. When her father took her to the hospital emergency room, it was too late. She died in an oxygen tent.

No one suggested that her parents were at fault. They cherished her as much as they were capable of cherishing anything and did for her all they could think of doing. In my opinion, Becky, as a result of severe retardation, simply was not equipped to live, which makes her story, for me, even more harrowing than Jonathan's.

The saddest of all the cases I have been involved in, however, is that of a boy I'll call Charles. He was nine months old when I first saw him. Up to the age of five months he had been a glowingly happy baby with bright blue eyes, vivid red hair and, having been born on Halloween, the nickname Pumpkin. He was constantly rolling around in his playpen, tossing toys about, almost getting up to sitting position all by himself and frequently crowing aloud for pure joy of life. At nine months he was an utterly different person.

His mother, Judy, told me how gradual the change had been.

"Our next-door neighbor is a good friend and used to come over here several times a day. She went off on a two-week vacation and came right over to tell me about it as soon as she returned. We were sitting in the living room. Charles was in the playpen in the middle of the room. Polly suddenly went silent and stared at him.

" 'What's happened?' she asked. 'Is he sick?'

"He was lying there on his back, gazing at the ceiling. I suddenly realized that I had seen him doing that several times in the last few days. He was eating and sleeping the same as ever, and there were still times when he moved around a lot and made a lot of noise. But he was quiet more often than he had been.

"I thought it probably was a natural stage for him to go through. But it was nearly time for his six-month checkup, so I made an appointment to take him in."

At that point the pediatrician was not much concerned. But up to then Charles had been gaining steadily in pounds and inches. In the following month he gained not an ounce, and Judy realized that he had completely stopped rolling over and kicking his legs, one of his favorite exercises. The pediatrician ordered a neurological examination.

The neurologist's verdict made Judy feel better. She had decided that the trouble might be a brain tumor, and he assured her there was no evidence of anything like that. What concerned him was that Charles seemed to be "going backward in time," as he put it, something he had never encountered before. He urged Judy to take the baby to a big medical center in a nearby city.

The tests took ten days, all of which Judy spent with Charles in the hospital. They were for her a descent into the kind of hell which can be created only by modern medicine at its very worst. None of the many physicians, technicians, and others who participated was cruel or even unkind to her, but the whole process could not have been more hurtful if it had intentionally been made so.

"Maybe the worst that happened," she told me, "was that

before it was over I actually got used to hearing Charles scream. They did blood test after blood test on him—and spinal taps, muscle biopsies, X-rays. They poked and prodded him in teams. Dozens of them. Maybe more than a hundred altogether. He had something rare so they all wanted to practice on him.

"My husband came down for the first weekend. By Saturday afternoon he couldn't take it anymore. He went home. I didn't blame him. I wanted to go with him. But I couldn't bear to leave the baby alone in that place."

When the last test had been evaluated, several specialists met with Judy and explained that Charles had an only recently identified disease of the nervous system, a progressive degeneration, probably as a result of some genetic inheritance not yet understood. There was no cure. The only outcome would be death, probably within a couple of years or so. To learn more about the disease they wanted her permission to take a sample of his brain tissue, though they had to tell her that it would do him no good.

"He's had enough tests," Judy told them. "You can examine his brain tissue after—after—"

They went on to tell her that they were fairly sure the disease was hereditary and that there was a fifty-fifty chance that, if she got pregnant again, the new baby would develop the same symptoms. There was no way of predicting in advance whether a child would have the disease. Amniocentesis would not spot it.

"I can't take a chance like that," Judy told me. "I'll never have another baby."

By the time I saw her for the first time, she had wept herself dry and was beginning to put some emotional distance between herself and what was left of Charles. She no longer called him Pumpkin. But she desperately wanted to do everything she could to make what was left of his life as comfortable as possible.

He was then, as I've said, nine months old. His muscle tone

was quite good, and he could sit in a high chair, eat from a spoon, and sometimes would hold his bottle with both hands while he sucked from it. I started them off with a variety of exercises to help keep his joints limber, and she experimented until she found that after his bath was the best time for him to work on these.

His response was great. He seemed to enjoy the exercises, stayed quite limber, and gained a little strength. At one point, indeed, I began to fear that Judy might be encouraged in false hopes. I had read the report of the results of his tests and knew that there simply was not any hope in the long run.

But all possibility of hope ended when Charles at about eleven months had his first seizures. They were much like the grand mal seizures of epilepsy. He had to be given drugs to control these, and the drugs made him so floppy that we could no longer do anything about helping him maintain muscle tone.

That was two years ago. My visits have slowly dwindled to one a month, that one chiefly for the purpose of helping Judy feel sure that she is doing all she can, which is very little. Now small, thin, and stiff, Charles sleeps all but five or six hours a day and spends those hours propped in a corner of the living room couch. He no longer seems to hear or see anything and is silent and immobile except when a seizure breaks through the barrier of the drugs he is given.

There is no evidence that he is suffering any pain. All he seems to have left to lose is the ability to suck. When that is gone, it will take tube feeding to keep him alive. He eventually will stop having seizures and sink into a coma.

Judy's mother stays with him for a few hours every day, and Judy works part time in a bank, chiefly in an attempt to find some new interests. It is not a very successful effort. Her true occupation is, simply, waiting. When the end does come, her reward will be sorrow and regret. She has done nothing to deserve so bleak a fate, but only after her waiting ends can she hope to start living a new life.

8

A Fortunate Handicap

A Neglected Child with a Deformed Arm
Finds a Loving Home

CHILD ABUSE has been a fashionable subject lately in movies and on television shows. I think it is a good thing to bring it out in the open rather than sweep it under the rug, but my own work has yet to involve me with a single clear-cut case of it. I say "clear-cut" because I have encountered several different degrees of child neglect and, if the neglect is severe enough, it obviously amounts to abuse. That's what one of our state laws so declares. But deciding just when neglect must be judged that severe is no simple matter.

Clover, the child with the severe case of cerebral palsy, certainly needed far more care and attention than she got. Yet her mother could not be accused of neglecting her. Poor Norene was so defeated that she had very little of anything to give anyone. She tried to do for Clover what little she was capable of doing.

The neglect was worse in the case of Mindy, the heroine of this chapter. Yet it never was possible to bring formal charges of child abuse against her parents, nor am I quite certain they were morally guilty. What's more, the story has a happy ending. It is quite a story.

Born four weeks early, Mindy came with an assortment of problems and one severe handicap. The latter was her left arm. The shoulder and elbow were of normal shape, though

126

noticeably smaller than her right shoulder and elbow, but the left forearm tapered to a knobby bulb from which three small, fingerlike appendages dangled. No one has been able even to guess whether the explanation of it involved her genes or something that happened while her mother was carrying her.

Her other problems were more generalized. According to one of the nurses who had helped care for her at the hospital where she was born, she was the most irritable baby the nurse ever had worked with. She was prone to diaper rash, had severe colic, was allergic to milk and many other common allergens, and was highly susceptible to infections, especially colds.

Because of her deformed arm, the people at the hospital decided that I might be of use to her and made an appointment for me to see her at home when she first went there at the age of about two months. That appointment and a couple of others were canceled when she had to go back to the hospital, once because of prolonged vomiting, another time with high fever and dehydration, and a third with a kidney infection. When I at last did get to her home, she was four months old.

The house was in the poorest section of a small city, and the directions provided by Mindy's mother, Margie, proved remarkably vague. The family had lived there only a short time, and no one in the neighborhood seemed to have heard of them. By knocking on half a dozen doors I finally found someone who recognized the street name Margie had given me as that of a half-block-long, unpaved alley. When I found the house, I couldn't get out of my car because two huge, ferocious dogs rushed up and repeatedly lunged at my door, promising quite convincingly to tear me limb from limb if I opened it.

I beeped my horn until Margie opened her back door, then rolled my window down a couple of inches and screeched out my identity. She managed to drag one dog to a post and tie him there. When she could not collar the other, she picked up a chunk of wood and urged me out of the car.

"He don't bite, but I'll be ready if he tries."

While she held him at bay, I scurried into the house through a back porch replete with garbage, broken furniture, car parts, and dirty diapers. The kitchen featured a filthy stove with an oven door held partly closed by a wire attached to a nail driven in the wall. There was also a table laden with pans of food I could not recognize and guessed must be for the dogs. The living room was tiny, dark, and crowded with a grimy couch, chair, table, and kerosene burning heater. The stench kept bringing me close to gagging.

As we walked into the living room, a toddler in urine-soaked pajamas came out of a bedroom on the far side.

"Oogie, oogie," he said, reaching for my bag of toys.

"No, Bobby, no!" Margie yelled at him, slapping his hands down. "Get out of here. I'll give you something to eat."

It was about eleven in the morning, and apparently this older child, nearly two years old, was still unfed and unchanged. Margie spent only a few moments in the kitchen with him, then returned and fetched Mindy from the bedroom.

I had to blink back tears at that first sight of her and not primarily because of her arm. She was miserably scrawny and anxious, had almost continuous diaper rash from navel to knees, and badly needed a bath and to have her nose and ears cleaned. Her movements were jerky, at times seeming to be little more than involuntary twitches. Her cry was high-pitched and nasal, more like that of a newborn than a four-month-old. She obviously was unused to being handled but calmed down a little when I rocked her for a while.

"Does she seem as active as Bobby when he was a little baby?" I asked.

"Naw, she don't do nothing but mess her pants and scream. And get sick."

"Is she cuddly? Does she like to be held a lot?"

"I don't fuss with her much. Anyways, she likes it in her room. I just prop her bottle up and let her take what she wants."

"She's kind of young to take a bottle that way." I started to get sharp but caught myself. My first responsibility was to try to get Margie to help Mindy, and anger would do no good. "I'd like to see how she sucks. Is it time for her to eat yet?"

"She'll eat any time. I'll get her bottle." She brought it from the bedroom. "Well, she didn't eat much of it last night. I heard her fussing but I figured it was just that colic." She handed the bottle to me.

"I think we'd better get her a fresh one," I said, fighting to keep the anger out of my voice. "This one could have gone bad during the night. It could make her sick."

Margie opened it and sniffed at it.

"It's the awful soy bean stuff. Never does smell good." But she moved toward the kitchen, and I followed.

Bobby was kneeling on the table, eating from one of the pots of unidentifiable stuff. Margie ignored him, emptied Mindy's bottle in the sink, and got out a can of soy bean milk to refill it.

"Let me wash that for you," I said as pleasantly as I could manage. The nipple was caked with solidified formula, and both it and the bottle took a lot of scrubbing. When I finally got it clean and refilled, Mindy gulped down a couple of ounces. I had to pry the nipple loose in order to burp her. She spit up a little food along with a burp.

"That stuff costs money," said Margie, "and she's always wasting it like that."

I could see no point in trying to start Mindy on a physical therapy program until I could persuade Margie to give her at least a minimum of thought and attention. The best way I could think of to encourage this was to tell her, as if it were a sort of prescription, that she must hold Mindy in her arms and feed her fresh formula from a clean bottle once every four hours during the day. She also must change Mindy's diapers right away after every bowel movement and at least once every couple of hours. To give it some force, I told her that a nurse would be calling at the house regularly to "help" her with all this.

My first act after I left was to find a phone and call the public health nurse assigned to that neighborhood. She understood the situation at once and promised to drop in on Margie. By taking along disposable diapers, a few cans of the soy milk formula, and something for the rash she would be able to ingratiate herself. She would see to it that the children got their necessary immunizations and would try to get them and Margie to the well-baby clinic.

Then I called the social worker our agency had assigned to Mindy's case and reported my observations. He sighed. I sighed. We talked about neglect and abuse and the law and the law's ambiguities and differences in life styles. He said it was a good thing I would be there every week to "monitor the situation." I said he had better get there himself so that he could back me up if I eventually had to file a report of child abuse. He also could help me make Margie understand that there was a lot our agency might be able to do for Mindy and her family. If she did not realize this and if I seemed a nuisance, what was to stop her from telling me to go away and leave her alone? He promised to do all he could.

He also gave me a little background information on Margie and her husband, Don. Both were children of broken homes, had dropped out of high school early, had been drifting around from town to town for several years, and were in their twenties. They had been married shortly after Bobby was born. Currently, Don had a part-time job in a cattle feedlot where he did the dirtiest of the dirty work.

It seemed to me one of the most miserable ways of life imaginable. I knew it would seem the same to almost everyone I knew. Obviously, I was going to have to make a great effort if I wanted to get a glimpse of how it seemed to Margie.

When I arrived for my second visit, my good intentions almost went down the drain. The stench had been a complete surprise the first time I was there. This time anticipation made its effects on me worse for a little while. Twice, I started to gag. Fortunately, Margie's attention was away from me both times, and I was able to get my nausea under control before she noticed.

There were a few noticeable improvements, though. The supply of disposable diapers furnished by the public health nurse had made Margie willing to change both children more often. Also, Mindy's rash was a little improved as a result of the nurse's efforts. But Mindy remained extremely irritable, easily startled, and set off into inconsolable crying. I tried to comfort her with cuddling and to explain to Margie about her need for such reassurance.

"She's just a spoiled brat," was Margie's response. "All that attention in the hospital. She don't know how to take care of herself."

That remark left me stunned for a moment. I felt disoriented. It flashed through my mind that it could be the punch line for some very sick joke.

When I recovered, I yearned for an inspiration about how to jolt Margie into looking at things from Mindy's point of view. None came.

"She's only four months old," was the best I could do. "The only way she has to take care of herself is by crying to let you know that she needs your help."

That made no impression at all. The only other gambit that occurred to me was to show Margie the soft pompom I had brought for her to stroke Mindy with. I tried to explain how this could stimulate Mindy's awareness of different parts of her body and perhaps eventually get her to try using the three rudimentary fingers on her malformed arm. A loud crash in the kitchen changed the subject.

"Bobby! You cut that out!" Margie screamed. And I mean screamed. The noise made my ears ring.

"That damn kid," she said to me. "He's always looking for

something to eat. Found him on the back porch eating the dogs' food this morning."

"But if he's hungry, Margie, you ought to feed him." I tried to be reasonable.

"Aw, we had a big dinner last night. And Don don't get paid till tomorrow. We gotta make do till then."

"You mean you don't have any food in the house?"

"I got a little beans left, I guess. We'll probably eat after Don gets home. I don't eat in the daytime much."

I had seen many empty soft drink cans scattered around inside and outside the house. I tried to tell her that a child Bobby's age needed a varied diet and at least three meals a day.

"Don and me never had three meals in one day our whole life. We eat when we feel like it. When we got something to eat."

She was simply doing unto her children what had been done unto her. The possibility of doing otherwise had not occurred to her. I asked her about food stamps. On their income, I knew, they certainly would be eligible for these.

"You mean stamps like for letters?" was Margie's puzzled reply. She had never heard of food stamps. Apparently, she had almost no contact of any kind with anyone except her husband and children.

The public health nurse, the social worker, and I got together that afternoon. They agreed that the family's eating habits were a good starting point for our efforts to improve things for the children. In addition to arranging for food stamps we tried to work out our schedule of visits for maximum effectiveness. The nurse could see them twice a week and the social worker and I once each, and we chose our different days. We agreed to try to make our visits at noon and to arrive with some food which we would help Margie prepare for herself and the older child and some sort of baby food with which to vary Mindy's diet.

These were, of course, weak stratagems with which to make

up to Margie for the neglect that had been her lot in her own childhood. They made some differences, though. We soon could see that she was feeding the children more often even when we were not there. But I'm not sure she was convinced there was good reason for doing so. If she had felt a bit stronger, had had a little more confidence in herself, she probably would have preferred to tell us to go away and leave her alone.

I plugged away at physical therapy for Mindy and kept showing Margie little games she could play with the baby that would help develop what muscles she did have in the incomplete arm. Now and then Margie seemed to get interested and would watch carefully what I did and try to imitate me a few times while I was there. But I never saw evidence in Mindy's behavior that Margie had made any attempt to keep up these activities between my visits.

So what was I going to do about that? Without a lot of help from someone day in and day out, Mindy was going to grow up much more severely handicapped than if she got that help. But my opinion was not grounds for filing formal charges of neglect against Margie.

It was the social worker who stumbled on the solution to our problems. The agency has a service called respite care which it can offer to the parents of handicapped children. Full-time care of an ordinary infant occasionally exhausts even a competent and devoted mother, and a baby with problems naturally makes more demands. To provide a little time off, the agency pays foster parents, whom it registers and monitors, to take such children into their homes for from a weekend to a couple of weeks.

When told about this, Margie was suspicious at first, not to say incredulous, but soon shrugged off her doubts and accepted the offer. She was told that the foster home could keep Mindy and Bobby for a week, and she seemed to accept and understand this. She was supposed to call for the children at the foster home at the end of the week. Her not showing up on schedule was half expected. Next day the social worker went looking for her, could find no sign of life around the house, and was informed by Don's employer that Don had not been seen for days and would not be taken back if he ever should return. Neither Margie or Don has been seen or heard from since.

Whatever legal or moral judgments may be passed on them, they probably did the best thing they could for Mindy and Bobby. The children stayed a couple of weeks longer in the respite care home and then went to permanent foster parents, whom I shall call Lisa and Harry. They have two sons of their own, five and seven years old, want more children, and have been told Lisa can bear no more because of complications that developed after the birth of the second son.

"Harry's a policeman," Lisa told me on my first visit to Mindy in her new home, "and he knew there are children who need homes and never enough homes to go around. I felt uneasy about being paid to be a mother, but when I found out that the money would barely cover food and clothing, I knew I wanted to do it."

Soon after I arrived, Bobby woke from his nap in his room and called "Mamma, Mamma." I had never before heard him say that word. Lisa went and fetched him cuddled in her arms, and he looked as if he felt he was in paradise.

Mindy still was irritable but noticeably less so.

"She gets worked up fast," Lisa said. "I try to be ready with her bottle when she's hungry and I get her into bed as soon as she lets me know she's tired. Otherwise, it's almost no time before she's at the point where she can't be comforted. She just cries and cries to break your heart."

There obviously was nothing Lisa needed to learn about mothering. If anyone could do it, she was the one to make up for what Margie had been unable to do for those children. Indeed, she seemed capable of making up for generations of poor mothering or lack of mothering. Considering the life

Margie apparently had lived, that might be exactly what Lisa was in the process of doing.

She wanted to know how I thought the arm would affect Mindy's future, whether there would be a lot of activities closed to her because of it, and whether anything could be done to help her get ready for the way other children would stare and ask questions.

"Matthew, my five-year-old," she told me, "asked me if Mindy's other hand would come in the mail. He thinks it got broken off."

I was able to tell her about several other children I had worked with who had limbs missing or malformed. One of the most pertinent stories was what the mother of one such child told me about her own reaction when a friend, seeing the child for the first time, had said, "Poor thing!"

"Poor thing, hell," had been the mother's reaction. "He's rich. He's got us."

By "us" she meant his large family of parents, grandparents, brothers, and sisters. I felt sure that Mindy's new family was going to be the source of exactly the kind of security she will need to develop the confidence that she can do what she wants to do. She will have the strength she will need to withstand the casual cruelty of the insensitive.

Eventually, a pediatrician would set up an appointment for Mindy to be examined at a university medical center which has a program for young amputees. There it could be decided if and when she can use an artificial hand or some other prosthesis. But for the time being the important thing was to work to compensate both for the malformed arm and the lack of stimulation and encouragement in her early months.

For a six-month-old she was noticeably delayed in her development in ways that should not have been affected by the condition of her arm. She tended to lie inert much of the time because that was what Margie had wanted and encouraged her to do. Hugging, cuddling, games of peekaboo, and such, all of which came to Lisa instinctively, were the best possible ways to overcome that passivity and get Mindy started trying to see what she could do.

I remember saying at that first visit that she should be doing a lot of kicking while she lay on her back. She also should now and then try to use her good hand to bring one foot or the other up to her face for examination. Lisa had seen her do only a little weak kicking and no pulling at her feet with her hand.

By chance it was two weeks before I could get back for my second visit. When I arrived, Lisa had Mindy on a blanket on the floor. She was alternating between vigorous kicking out and pulling one foot up to her face. And, best of all, she was laughing out loud. It was like a textbook demonstration of the effectiveness of good mothering.

From that point on my contribution was mostly help in stimulating what there was of Mindy's left arm and watching for signs of her developing balance problems. She was going to have to work out her own ways of compensating for the imbalance in her upper body. The important thing was to make sure she didn't go about it in a way that would produce a spinal curve or other unnecessary impairment.

One technique, as usual, was a lot of stroking of the arm with objects of varied textures. And I suggested that Lisa gently stimulate the fingerlike appendages at the end of the arm as often as she could find the time—pulling at them, nibbling, sucking, and whatever else she could think of. This would compensate to some extent for the feedback not available from the missing parts of the arm.

When Mindy began trying to push up her head and chest while lying prone, we made a little platform topped by a soft cushion for her to rest her left elbow on. This made it possible for her to get the same distance off the floor on both sides. Before long, she was getting up on her right hand, left elbow plus platform, and knees, then rocking back and forth.

By her first birthday she and her family were taking her

incomplete left arm for granted. She distinguished herself at the party by plunging into her cake with both arms. Her foster father took a great picture of her licking the frosting off the end of her shortened limb.

A couple of months later she pulled herself up to standing at the couch for the first time and, cruising sideways toward her good side, took her first steps. Within a few days she could cruise the other way, too, and she soon went on to toddle a few steps toward the nearest chair, lower herself to the floor, crawl the rest of the way to her destination, then pull herself up again.

Just what sort of artificial hand or arm Mindy will get still remains to be decided. She makes a lot of use of her left arm as it is. For instance, if she wants to work on some object with her right hand, she holds it against her left side with her left elbow. Probably because she is always trying things like this, she seems to be developing strength and flexibility in the "fingers" at the end of the arm. The prosthesis expert at the medical center is fascinated and wants to see how much she can learn to do with them before trying to design anything for her.

As of this writing it seems likely that, though they may never realize it, both she and her brother always will have reason to be grateful for the incompleteness of her left arm. Had she been born without visible physical handicap, no outsiders would have taken special interest in her. The two of them would have grown up in abject misery, and they probably would have become, if they survived, new editions of their unloved and unloving parents. Instead, their lives are so happy and full of promise that the sorrow in which they began may eventually even fade out of their nightmares, because now their foster parents plan to adopt them formally when the red tape spun by the disappearance of Margie and Don can be untangled.

9

Sometimes a Sound from the Silence

Three Autistic Children

THE TERM autism is derived from the Greek word *autos*, meaning self, and is defined as "abnormal subjectivity." In 1943 Leo Kanner of Johns Hopkins University launched its current usage as a word for a syndrome displayed by certain children. Some authorities list up to forty symptoms as sometimes part of this syndrome, but it has a fairly simple basic definition: almost total withdrawal from involvement with others, such as avoidance of eye contact and refusal to speak, plus refusal to take the usual interest in objects. When an autistic child does take notice of some object, it is likely to be in a compulsive way involving long repeated stroking, scratching, spinning, or other such manipulation of it.

No genetic abnormality has yet been found to be involved in such behavior. It used to be thought that it was caused by extreme parental coldness, but the facts do not agree. Autistic children turn up even in warm and loving families. Neither has there been any evidence that brain damage is a factor. About the only thing agreed on in the way of explanation, though it does not really explain much, is that these children seem to react to stimuli quite differently from the rest of us.

They are by no means all alike, however. Bernard Rimland of the Institute for Child Behavior Research in San Diego has assembled from forty countries the case histories of some 5,400 autistic children. In an article in *Psychology Today* (September, 1979) he reported that 531 of these showed extraordinary abilities, such as being able to multiply in their heads, almost instantly, two four-figure numbers, or to identify quickly and accurately the day of the week on which some monthly date fell far in the past or will fall far in the future. What makes these abilities truly extraordinary is that in almost all other respects these children seem severely retarded. Indeed, they usually are called idiot savants.

Rimland suggests that they might better be called autistic savants and outlines his hypothesis that what enables them to perform their strange feats, and at the same time leads to their withdrawal from most or all ordinary human contacts and concerns, is profound and habitual concentration on some narrow subject. They are, that is, super-specialists, not merely unwilling but actually unable to take a broad view of anything. Supporting this hypothesis, according to Rimland, is the fact that a number of autistic savants have outgrown their autism and, in the process, lost their extraordinary abilities.

Those having such abilities, of course, are only a tiny minority of the children who display the syndrome of autism. None of the few cases I have worked with has shown, to my knowledge, any sort of extraordinary ability. Still, the existence of autistic savants has to be of great interest to anyone who works with children of this kind. Such children usually seem, and according to most tests results have to be classified as, quite retarded, but often there is something about them that sets them apart from most other children so classified.

In the case of the one autistic child with whom I have done a good deal of work, that something was the way she once in a while would suddenly and briefly abandon her withdrawal and open up to me and the rest of the world around her. This had on me an effect like that of the sun coming out from behind dark clouds. But it was only after many months of work that she reached this stage.

The first time I saw Beth she had wrapped herself tightly around her mother's trunk and buried her face against her mother's shoulder. Ellen, the mother, looked miserable and defeated. A pediatrician had referred her to the agency I work with, and a social worker had told me that Beth was twenty months old, spoke not at all, walked just a little, and seemed very remote and frightened. A tentative diagnosis of autism had been discussed with the parents. Although the term meant little to them, Ellen and her husband, Jack, were well aware that something was badly wrong with Beth and were grateful for any help. They had three other children—boys of ages seven, nine, and ten—and were stretched near their limits by them and the struggle to keep a small gardening business going. The additional problem of Beth's differentness seemed to overwhelm them.

At my suggestion Ellen and I sat on the floor of the living room, Beth still clinging tightly to her mother. My usual entertainments and diversions were of no use. Wind-up toys, puppets, books—Beth would not turn her head to look at anything I offered. Imitations of cats, dogs, birds, and motors also went unnoticed.

Eventually, I gave up and sat talking quietly with Ellen. After a few minutes of this Beth slowly relaxed her hold so that her mother could move her to her lap. She still kept her face against her mother but now made her first movements, which consisted of picking at the little fuzz balls on Ellen's woolen sweater. This at least made it obvious that she could see reasonably well. I asked about her hearing.

"It's kind of crazy," Ellen said. "I've seen her turn her head to look at a fly buzzing against a window behind her when I could just barely hear the buzz myself. But once I was baking a pizza and forgot about it and the smoke alarm went off. We all jumped up and ran around and yelled at each other about what to do. Beth just sat there in her high chair, swinging a chain back and forth, back and forth. She didn't pay any attention to the commotion. She could have been stone deaf, except I'm sure she isn't."

By this time Ellen had eased Beth to the floor where she sat staring at a toy xylophone belonging to one of her brothers. Suddenly—though the movement was really quite slow, it was so unexpected that I involuntarily pulled back a little—she took her mother's hand, closed the fingers around the xylophone stick, and moved the hand so that it struck four notes at random. Then she dropped the hand and stared at the wall in front of her.

The effect was eerie. Could she be trying to tell us something? Something strange and wonderful? Something about how her attention was being held captive?

I moved a little closer with the idea of letting her get used to my looks, sounds, smells. Ellen started telling me about how Beth had been such a wonderful baby, only cried when she was hungry, went right to sleep when placed in her crib, never fussed. While she was talking, Beth reached for my hand, moved it to the stick, and again struck the xylophone. Only three notes this time.

I was pleased and excited. Ellen shot me down in a hurry.

"She'll use anybody's hand that's there when she wants to do something like that. Doesn't seem to matter whether it's me or a stranger."

This included only large, quiet, slow-moving strangers, however. Ellen said that Beth seemed to turn herself off completely in the presence of other children and any adults who were noisy or moved around much. She also would have nothing to do with dogs or cats or even the smallest, most cuddly kittens or puppies.

The agency that sent me to Beth had no one else to offer who had any more knowledge than I of autism, so there was nothing for me to do but take the plunge. In the following week I re-read everything on the subject in my notes and library and looked up all the more recent reports I could find, including two books written by parents of autistic children who had devoted long years to working with their offspring. The best that came of all this was confirmation that the most promising approach to Beth probably would be the same gentle stroking of the skin I used with many other handicapped infants to try to attract their attention to various parts of their bodies.

With Beth, though, I feel that it would not do for me to try to perform the stroking myself, at least at the beginning. She might submit but be driven to even further withdrawal of her attention. So on my second visit I showed Ellen how to stroke her, using a soft wash cloth.

At first Beth's reaction was her usual inattention, but after several minutes work on her arms and back and shoulders she began to pay a little heed, glancing out of the corner of her eye toward the part of her body being stroked. When Ellen moved down to her legs and feet, Beth actually withdrew them, almost a small triumph for us. I suspect that the soles of her feet are ticklish, so that she simply cannot ignore you when you stroke them. That may have been a clue to a way of drawing her out still further, but I never dared work too hard at it for fear of making her feel attacked.

I also persuaded Ellen to resume trying simple baby games with Beth, the kind of thing most parents start doing spontaneously with a baby at four or five months when it can show pleasure and excitement. You wiggle your fingers and slowly move them up the child's arm or leg or tummy and end with a gentle tickle. Ellen had played such games with all her children in their infancy but had long since given up trying to interest Beth in them.

Another project was getting the whole family to take turns dancing with her. Ellen and Jack could start by holding her close, then experiment with lifting her over their heads, on their shoulders, even upside down. Her brothers held her by the hands and wiggled and bounced around. When she insisted on stopping, they stopped, but often she seemed willing and perhaps even glad to go on and on.

Over a period of a year she surprised us many times. Once in a while she would hold out an arm to me to be stroked or take the cloth and rub her own leg. Once she took my hand to show that she wanted me to play a tickle game on her tummy. Another time Ellen saw her play a tickle game on one of her dolls. These were rare little triumphs, though, seeming like brief escapes from the dungeon to which she had been apparently condemned.

When she was about three, she started school in a class for children with multiple handicaps. Her teacher made a nook for her where she could be left in safety when the adults present were working with the other five children in the class. Teaching Beth was strictly a one-on-one undertaking.

That teaching made an indisputable difference in the course of the next year. Beth seemed to grow so accustomed to other children that she would let them take her by the hand and walk around the room. Even more striking was her playground behavior. There she got in the habit of approaching an adult, looking up imploringly, and reaching up with her arms. This resulted, of course, in a lot of hugs and cuddling, and it seemed a tremendous breakthrough that she should not just accept these but actively seek them.

The teacher noticed, though, that Beth was completely indiscriminate. She would approach any adult at all when the spirit moved her—the familiar teacher or a total stranger, male or female, a person who responded warmly or someone who picked her up in only a perfunctory way. In other words, it never was clear whether what she wanted was to be hugged and cuddled or just to be lifted up in the air out of range of the other children.

Still, even that was at least a little better than simply withdrawing all her attention from the world around her, and there were a few signs that she was developing genuine interest in other children and was able to have and express feelings about them. Once she stroked a crying classmate's head. Another time she stamped a foot at a child who tried to take away her snack. And she would occasionally mimic the actions of other children: covering a doll with a blanket, putting on a hat, drinking out of a doll's teacup.

She was a little past four when her family moved away. The only news I've had is a Christmas card from Ellen enclosing a photograph of Beth holding a kitten. She is looking off to the side, but she also is quite unmistakably smiling. How much my efforts helped to bring her that far, and whether she will progress any further, I probably never shall know.

The two other possibly autistic children I want to mention were sent to me because of the same odd symptom—they walked on their toes. This is not necessarily a sign that something is wrong. Although I have seen no statistical studies, I suspect that in most cases it is merely a habit a child gets into when first learning to walk and then gradually outgrows in a few weeks or months. On the other hand, it can be an indication of some physical handicap, such as a congenitally short Achilles tendon. To the best of my knowledge, however, its connection with symptoms of autism is strictly coincidental.

Lance was a little over two when his pediatrician referred him to me. He was only a part-time tiptoer, easily bringing his heels to the floor when he wanted to but frequently going all the way up onto the tips of his big toes, ballet style. Although he was not as withdrawn as Beth, he was decidedly enough so to make one think of autism. His mother, a whirlwind of energy with three part-time jobs, could take him with her anywhere and simply plunk him down with a few of his toy cars. He would sit and spin a wheel for an hour or more at a time, occasionally making little motor sounds to himself and uttering an appropriate word, such as car, truck, or go.

One of my stratagems for helping him outgrow tiptoeing was to fit him with a pair of plastic roller skates and turn him loose in a room with deep, soft shag carpeting. It was impossible even for him to go on his toes on roller skates, and he seemed to enjoy lunging around heels down and not to mind falling down once in a while. But neither this nor anything else I could think of dissuaded him from tiptoeing when he was able to and felt like it.

An orthopedist had a little more success, but only a little. He put Lance in short leg casts for six weeks. When the casts came off, Lance walked quite normally for a couple of weeks. Then he started going back up on his toes.

Not long after this he was sent off to spend the summer on his grandparents' ranch. I did not see his mother again until late in the fall, when we chanced to meet in the local public library. Lance, she assured me, was cured. How?

"His grandfather bought him a pair of cowboy boots and told him that cowboys never walk on their toes."

I don't know if that really is the whole story, but neither do I know any reason why it cannot be. From one of Lance's teachers at a nursery school I have heard that he walks quite normally now. He still is able to turn inward and ignore everything around him when he feels like doing so, but there are other times when he seems fairly outgoing.

My other tiptoer who also had some symptoms of autism was a remarkably pretty little girl with curly dark hair, pale skin, and deep blue eyes. Kari had an intense stare and always seemed to be concentrating hard on whatever she was looking at, though I often felt she was looking right through me. A little over three years old when she was referred to me, she walked quite normally much of the time, but once in a while she would pause, rise slowly onto her toes, stay on them until she again came to a stop, then slowly lower her heels.

Her mother, Barbara, was also pretty and quiet. She kept herself and Kari beautifully groomed and, from the way she handled her daughter, certainly seemed to enjoy contact with her. On my first visit she was holding Kari in her lap while we chatted. Kari picked up her hand and moved it to a wind-up toy in the shape of a dog. Barbara wound it, and Kari watched with rapt attention until the dog's tail stopped wagging, then moved Barbara's hand to it again.

Left to herself, Kari would sit and stare into space without moving for ten or fifteen minutes at a stretch. Yet when I fitted her with roller skates she seemed to watch the process with great interest, and she quite willingly, though very solemnly, trudged back and forth across the rug in them. During the six months I worked with her there were periods when she gave up tiptoeing for days at a stretch, but she always went back to it again. She also got to be more active physically, learning to ride a tricycle and to climb and slide down a slide, sometimes in the company of two neighborhood children her own age.

All this time I heard from her at most only a rare monosyllable, usually a "no." Then one day when I sat down to play with her she said: "Where's the box? The one with all the pieces? I want to do the puzzle."

It was almost like hearing a statue speak. Even Barbara had only heard her utter a single simple sentence at a time. Presumably she had suddenly arrived at some stage in her own unique maturation process.

Not long after that Barbara got a job and sent Kari, then just turned four, to a small private nursery school. After a couple of months I called to ask how she was doing.

"She loves it," Barbara told me. "She's learning to read, and her teacher's enthusiastic about her. Says Kari loves to do her work and is a good influence on the others. But you know, she still gets up on her toes once in a while. Usually gets back down again right away, though, without even taking a step. I guess there's no harm in it. She'll give it up when she's ready to."

As of this writing, there is a consensus of expert opinion that autism has organic rather than psychological causes. Intensive treatment of the symptoms sometimes results in considerable improvement, but often involves the cooperation of specially trained teachers, speech therapists, pediatricians, physical and occupational therapists, psychiatrists and, above all, parents dedicated to round-the-clock-and-calendar efforts. Even then, however, the child's relations with other people and the world in general often remain limited and awkward.

To put it simply, autism remains a haunting mystery.

10
Faith, Hope, and Unreality
A Microcephalic Child

Duncan was eight months old when I first saw him. He is microcephalic, meaning that his head is a little smaller than normal. It is not grotesquely small, just barely noticeably so, about two inches less in circumference than the normal minimum. The condition is rather rare, and why the skull fails to reach normal size is not known.

The effect, on the other hand, is known in detail. Because the brain cannot grow to full size, intelligence is limited, often quite severly so. In cases like Duncan's, the IQ limit is about 30. It is possible to toilet train such a boy eventually and to teach him to feed himself, to dress and undress himself, to speak and understand a few words, but not much more.

These are what I think of as the mechanical aspects of his potentialities. His personality, outlook, relations with his family and other people he meets depend on how he is treated. Acceptance of his limits and loving encouragement to do what he can produce results far different from merely efficient attention to his physical needs.

At my first meeting with Duncan and his mother, Marcia, I learned that he had been born in a city some distance away and that the family had moved to our town only a few weeks earlier. He was her third child and eleven years younger than his half-brother, Craig. His half-sister, Heidi, was fourteen. His father, Tyler, a traveling salesman, had adopted the two older children—Marcia's by a previous marriage—but he also wanted children of his own. Marcia told me that she already was pregnant with her fourth child.

147

The obstetrician who delivered Duncan should have noticed that his head was a bit small. For some reason he seemed not to have said anything to Marcia about it. Apparently, no one else had, either. At least, no one had said anything in a way to convince her that something was wrong.

"Duncan's good as gold," was her way of perceiving his lethargy. "He hardly ever cries, and he sleeps right through the night and takes a couple of long naps every day. He's just perfect."

It was Tyler, her husband, who eventually became uneasy and insisted, shortly after they moved to our town, that she take the child to a pediatrician. The latter saw at a glance what was wrong, suggested physical therapy, and referred her to the agency I work with. When I was asked to see Duncan, I got in touch with the pediatrician, and she told me what she had told Marcia. Otherwise I never would have known that she had even mentioned the small head. All that Marcia mentioned was that the doctor thought Duncan would benefit from physical therapy because it involved stimulation.

"Duncan's really just lazy," she assured me. "What he needs is a little push once in a while."

I tried to explain to her that there is no such creature as a lazy infant. We human beings are so constructed that we start testing and developing our physical, mental, and emotional equipment as soon as we are born. If a baby is not busy at this most of its waking time, there is something wrong, usually with the nervous system. Knowing that the pediatrician had tried to explain to Marcia about microcephaly, I probed as gently as possible to see what she had done with the information.

"Oh," she said, "so Duncan isn't going to be a genius. Who wants a genius around the house? He'll be plenty smart enough to suit me."

That should have alerted me to what I was up against, but I felt only faint misgivings. Her confidence, even if excessive, seemed at that stage far better than the fearful helplessness

I often have to deal with in similar cases. She certainly was willing to get down to the kind of work that could make a difference for Duncan, and it was high time to start.

At eight months he looked more like a four-month-old. He had large brown eyes, which he sometimes widened, and a slow, slight smile but hardly any other facial expression. When I moved a toy back and forth about a foot from his face, he focused on it and followed it a little way but never all the way from side to side as most babies half his age usually will. Nor did he roll over, sit with support, or hold his head steady. His muscle tone in general was extremely floppy so that when you held him in your arms he sagged like a bagful of sand.

After demonstrating and explaining these abnormalities to Marcia, I told her that we could help him compensate for them at least to some extent, and I explained how to give him tactile stimulation and what it might do for him. She was enthusiastic.

"Stimulation," she said. "That's just the thing. He's been such a sleepy baby. We'll wake him up and get him going."

Her tone worried me a little, so I took pains to urge her to be gentle with him. I used a soft cotton washcloth to rub his arms, legs, palms, soles, and back in my demonstration and explained that it would be a good idea to try other objects with nice, soft textures so long as he seemed to like them. I emphasized that she should not use anything that left his skin marked or reddened for more than a minute or so after she stopped massaging him.

When I returned for my second visit a week later, patches of skin here and there all over Duncan's body were red, rough, and scratched. Feeling both outraged and guilty, I asked what she had been doing to him. She showed me a nylon pot scrubber.

"Those soft things didn't get to him at all," she told me.

"But you've hurt him," I said, letting my indignation show. "You've hurt him badly. Surely he cried and fussed?"

"Oh some, some," said Marcia, letting my indignation slide right off her back as if she did not even notice it. "But it was good for him. He needed the stimulation. It really woke him up."

I realized then that her excessive confidence was the result of some sort of neurotic refusal to deal with the reality of Duncan's condition. Most of the rest of that session went into doing all I could to make her understand that she had done him far more harm than good. And thereafter I took care to spell out in detail every suggestion I offered her.

Over the next several months Duncan did make progress. One reason was that Marcia was quite able and willing to keep him with her most of the time around the house. Left alone in bed he would have vegetated. The moving about kept up a constant input which, little by little, made him a bit more alert to the world. Also, Marcia got it into her head that his involuntary movements had some intentional meanings, and this resulted in her repeating some things so often that meanings did seem to get through to him. During one period, for instance, she was quite sure that any slight movement he made with his arms was "waving bye-bye," and she responded by waving back and saying "bye-bye" so many times that at last he learned to do it on cue.

But the chief reason for his doing better was fourteen-year-old Heidi. A quietly unhappy and very thoughtful child, she jumped at the chance to earn a little of her mother's approval —plus a lot of mine—by working with Duncan. I soon found that I could suggest to her, or to Marcia in her presence, forms of massage or activities like rolling him back and forth in a blanket without fear they would be overdone to the point of harming him.

Observing the relationship between Heidi and Marcia also helped me to understand the latter a little better. The essence of her behavior is best described by the old-fashioned word "flighty." With only one exception that I ever observed, she constantly flitted from one thing to another and never got past the top layer of anything.

The exception was her certainty that Duncan was "going to be all right" as soon as this, that, or the other was done for him. Why she clung so tightly to this idea I never knew. Nothing I or anyone else said ever budged her from it, and all she would attend to in Duncan's behavior was evidence that he was improving in some way.

By the time he was fifteen months old there were a good many bits of such evidence, many of them the results of Heidi's efforts. If placed in a sitting position, he could hold it for a few minutes. With a lot of encouragement he would crawl a short distance commando style. He would sometimes pick up and mouth toys, hold his bottle for a few moments, accept food offered on a spoon, and sometimes hold and eat a cookie. Now and then he would coo vowel sounds or look in your direction if you spoke his name loudly and distinctly. Mostly, though, he just looked vacant.

And then his sister, Tina, was born. It was an event I had been looking forward to with hope. When she turned out to be a happy, attractive, and very active baby, I felt confident that my hopes soon would be realized. Marcia would simply have to come to her senses as soon as she recognized how much more rapidly than Duncan the new baby was developing and how many things she could do that her brother could not.

Instead, I learned from Heidi that Marcia said to her a few weeks after Tina's birth: "She'll be your baby. Duncan needs me. I just can't spend all that much time with Tina."

Not long after the occasion when Heidi told me this, Tyler was home between selling trips during one of my visits. He sat holding Tina and watching Marcia and me struggling with Duncan, who was taking very little interest in our efforts. Tyler suddenly got up, a look of sorrow on his face, and walked out of the room with Tina. He was such a decent man

—soft-spoken, easy-going, and remarkably tolerant of Marcia's vagaries—that I felt a great urge to help him by getting Marcia to face the facts about Duncan. I stopped what we were doing and tried once again to explain to her about the limits of his potentials.

"That may be the way it is according to the book," was the essence of her stubborn response, "but that's not the way it is with Duncan. You should see the wonderful things he does when everyone's gone and the house is quiet so he can concentrate."

She was simply unreachable.

The next development was the onset of her religious phase. With the simplicity and directness possible for the obsessed, she joined a church, took Duncan to the services, and asked the members of the congregation to pray for what she described as his recovery. A few weeks later she joined another church and did the same. Still later she added a third, and there may have been others I did not hear about.

Eventually, this culminated with her taking Duncan to a faith healer in the large city where he had been born. She knew that Tyler would strongly oppose this, so she told him nothing and arranged to make the trip while he was away for several days. Conscripting her seventy-three-year-old mother to supervise Heidi's care of the baby and try to ride herd on twelve-year-old Craig, she withdrew a large sum from the savings account she shared with Tyler, ordered Heidi to stay home from school with Tina, and was gone for three days. She announced on her return that marvelous things had happened, that Duncan soon would be well, and that all she had to do was listen to tape recordings she had bought, pray certain prayers at certain times of the day, and send more money to the healer so that he, too, would pray for Duncan.

In her absence Craig had set fire to brush in a nearby vacant lot, and the fire department had to be called. Explaining that to Tyler, along with Heidi's three-day absence from school and the bank account withdrawal, made it necessary for Marcia to tell all about her trip, too. And Tyler at last blew up. He raged at Marcia mostly about her neglect of Heidi, Craig, and Tina.

Marcia was contrite. Typically, however, her response to the neglect charge was to suggest that they find places to leave the children for a week while she and Tyler went off for a vacation. It turned out to be not a bad idea, though, and they came back from the trip happier and more in harmony with each other than at any time since I had met them.

That didn't last long. A couple of weeks after their return Marcia telephoned me. "Aren't there some special shoes," she wanted to know, "that would help Duncan learn to walk?"

At that point the commando crawl was still the best the child could do in the way of locomotion. Even when carefully arranged on hands and knees, he could not hold the position by himself for the briefest moment. The utter absurdity of Marcia's question suggested to me that she must be entering a new phase, and the suggestion proved correct.

She remained as obsessed as ever with Duncan. Continuing to ignore the other children, she neglected even routine immunizations for Tina and left her alone in a play pen or crib most of the time. Craig began an apprenticeship in delinquency and, when Tyler was home, did everything he could to provoke his stepfather in a desperate bid for attention. Heidi had the healthy instinct to involve herself in a lot of extracurricular activities at school so that she got home later and thus could be saddled with fewer responsibilities.

Marcia now tried to get her magical results with Duncan from technical equipment. After the special shoes came leg braces, glasses, hearing aids, a walker, parallel bars, and so on. Then she turned to megavitamins, carrot juice, and other nutritional experiments. Psychotherapy was the third stage. And through it all she shopped around among a variety of specialists ranging from neurosurgeons to chiropractors.

I know that more than one of those she consulted during this time suggested that she ought to talk with a counselor about her own problems. She blandly ignored all such hints. And she seemed to have no trouble holding to her contradictory convictions that, in the first place, there was nothing wrong with Duncan and, in the second place, she had just found the cure for what was wrong with him.

When he passed his third birthday, he became eligible for a day school for severely retarded children. He has daily physical therapy there and no longer needs me. Marcia, when we met on the street once after he had been attending the school for a few weeks, informed me that he was doing very well and that this proved she had been right all along about him. She had Tina with her on that occasion and seemed to take more interest in her than I had previously seen. Perhaps her obsession made her more uncomfortable than I knew and she has at last begun to find her way out of it.

I have included the story of Marcia and Duncan because it is the most outstanding example I know of a refusal to face reality. In the final chapter I have a good deal to say about facing reality in general, but right here I want to make a couple of points on the subject. If I did not do so it might be mistakenly assumed that I thought everything Marcia did was wrong.

I certainly do not mean to suggest that there is anything wrong with looking for help wherever you have hope of getting some. Marcia had a good instinct in seeking it from church groups. I remember one mother who was extremely reluctant to seek help for her severely handicapped daughter and, consequently, was nearing the end of her tether. One day she mentioned her despair to her minister. Within an hour he had four families volunteering to take the child for a day or two a week in order to give the mother some respite.

Nor do I mean that it is unrealistic to have any hopes at all for a severely limited child. I think often of the mother who, when told that her daughter probably would never develop beyond the mental and emotional level of a two-year-old, said: "Well, then, I want her to be the best two-year-old she can be."

But the most important thing about Marcia's story is what she did wrong. In allowing Duncan to dominate the family's life she did him no good at all. And she did all the others a great deal of wrong.

11
When a Mother Can't Cope
An Infant with Severely Limited Vision

Hoopla about medical miracles is not a new phenomenon. Some cavewoman probably started it all by boasting to her friends about what chewing willow bark had done for her and would do for them. And perhaps the most spectacular, not to say outrageous, medical publicity campaign of all time was launched in Germany at the Berlin Exposition of 1896 on behalf of what were then called "child hatcheries" for prematurely born infants. One of the greatest demonstrations ever of the natural affinity between show biz and health biz, this one made piles of money for exhibitors of "infant incubators with living infants." Their shows were sensations of most of the big international fairs from Berlin's in 1896 to Chicago's in 1932. According to A. J. Liebling, then *The New Yorker*'s reporter at large, the incubated infant exhibit at the Chicago World's Fair was outdrawn only by Sally Rand, the fan dancer.

Despite the commercialism, it is true that the invention of incubators saved the lives of many premature infants, among whom the mortality rate had been very high before that invention. As a result, incubators were installed in almost all hospitals with obstetrics wards by the end of the 1930s. Yet a dehumanizing rigidity was built into even the most respectable incubating centers that lasted unchallenged until the early 1960s.

Basically, an incubator for a premature infant is a glassed-in cage in which temperature, humidity, and oxygen concentration can be controlled. Even the most fragile babies have to

be taken out occasionally for feeding, bathing, diaper changing, and such, but until recently the removals were kept to a
minimum and done only by masked and rubber-gloved attendants who were instructed to work fast and not to indulge in
anything like cuddling or other such demonstrations of affection or concern. Rarely was a child's mother allowed to do
more than peek through the glass of the cage, and no other
member of its family got even a look into the room where the
cages were kept.

These inhuman practices resulted from what we now realize
was a profound misunderstanding of the relationship between
human beings and microorganisms. The efforts to prevent all
contact between the latter and premature infants were symptoms of germophobia. In the last quarter-century the medical
world has come to realize that premature babies are more subject than full-term ones to infection *because* of being separated
so soon from their mothers.

The fact is that, normally and naturally, each of us is a
walking home for countless viruses, bacteria, fungi, and such.
When all goes well, we are colonized by these tenants in our
infancy, the colonists migrating to us from our mothers. We
also receive from her the means of resisting over-multiplica-
tion of any one species of our tenants. If we do not get full
complements from mother, alien strains usually are waiting in
the wings to occupy the vacant niches, and in hospitals, where
most premature babies are born, there is high likelihood that
such aliens will be virulent.

While all this was becoming clear, other researchers were
studying the emotional effect of separating mother and child
at birth. The effect was bad. They discovered that an infant
needs its mother not only for her germs and resistance to
them but also for her love and frequent demonstrations of it.

Today, it seems almost incredible that it took "research" to
establish this as accepted medical doctrine, but fashions are as
powerful in this field as in clothing, marriage, language, and
such. In the 1920s, for instance, the book *Infant Care*, published by the U. S. Children's Bureau, then an unquestioned

authority for millions of parents, recommended that babies be fed only on schedule and sternly ignored if they cried between scheduled feedings. Twenty years later a new edition of the same book recommended that babies be fed on demand and only on demand.

Reports of this research on the emotional relationship between newborn infants and their mothers popularized the term "bonding." Babies, it was officially and scientifically pronounced, need to be cuddled by their mothers in order to develop emotional bonding to them. And then about ten years ago other researchers announced that they had found evidence that this works the other way, too. Mothers need to cuddle their babies in order to develop bonding to them.

Once this had been established by the rules of scientific evidence, it led to considerable effort to bring mother and premature infant together. When the baby is not only premature but also severely handicapped in a way that requires complicated intensive treatment and equipment, much separation still is inevitable. The result can be a sadly powerful demonstration of what happens when bonding does not develop.

Such a condition was demonstrated in the case of a patient of mine who was born two months early, weighed only two-and-a-half pounds, and had a hole in her heart. Her disability was a disappointing jolt for the mother, Vicki, and her husband, George. Married a little less than a year. they had looked forward eagerly to the baby's birth and the fuss to be made over them by relatives and friends. When immediately after birth the baby was whisked away by helicopter to a medical center two hundred miles away, they were crushed by a deep depression.

This was not because of naivete or inexperience. George was an accountant in a medical laboratory and had at least a little better than average understanding of what was being done for his daughter and why. Nor was the financial aspect a problem, his insurance covering all the costs. What hit them so hard was the abrupt disappearance of their baby into a sort of technological limbo.

Actually seeing her in that limbo helped a little, but only a little. As soon as Vicki was up to the trip, she and George drove to the medical center. Their baby was one of forty critically ill newborns in an intensive care unit where buzzers and other alarms sounded every few moments to alert the staff to fast developing crises. The new dispensation permitted Vicki to stroke the baby amid her engulfing respirator, heart monitor, intravenous feeding apparatus, catheter, and such. But a few months later Vicki still remembered that first visit and how she felt that "all those tubes were sucking the life out of my baby."

For three months the intensive care unit was the only place where the baby could be kept alive. The parents were first told that she had only a one-in-three chance of making it to three pounds, the size she had to reach before the surgeons would feel that they could do the operation to repair her heart. But after three weeks Vicki decided to go ahead and give her the name they had chosen—Amber Rose-Marie. It was a way of committing herself and, of course, made her vulnerable to the further jolts that came when Amber did gain the necessary weight. The operation repaired her heart but it stopped several times. Resuscitated, she developed pneumonia and for a few weeks had to have large amounts of oxygen to keep her blood well oxygenated.

During most of this time Vicki stayed in one of the rooms at the hospital provided for relatives of patients and was frequently encouraged to hold and cuddle Amber and, as soon as she was able to eat, to help feed her.

"But," Vicki told me later, "it didn't seem like she was really my baby. She belonged to the hospital, the nurses, the doctors, those awful machines."

Then Amber at last began gaining steadily, reached four pounds at three months, and was taken off the respirator. Two months later she weighed five-and-a-half pounds and was pronounced ready to go home. At the last conference with the hospital staff Vicki experienced the first hint of the final blow. Amber, someone told her and George, had "a moderate to severe visual defect." I feel fairly sure that long before then some physician must have tried to tell them about this possible consequence of the extra oxygen needed to save Amber's life but used terminology that made it possible for them to refuse to absorb what they were being told.

In any case, it was a subdued mother and father who drove home with their Amber, her heart now functioning normally but her eyes probably then perceiving only light and shadow and some outlines. How much vision she would ultimately have no one could say.

"All the time I was pregnant I kept thinking about coming home from the hospital with my baby," Vicki once told me. "And when Amber finally started gaining weight and stopped being critical, I started thinking about it again. But that day when we did come home, it wasn't like I thought it would be at all."

What she had expected was a great gathering of relatives and friends offering warmth and welcome and presents. What she came home to was an empty house and a demanding routine that began as soon as she walked through the door—a routine of mixing formulas, feeding the baby, changing her diapers, doing laundry, and trying to comfort an almost constantly restless, unhappy child.

As I have mentioned before, it is usual for friends and relatives to stay away from a family with a newborn known to have problems. Some feel embarrassed; some don't want to get involved; some think the parents need to be alone with their problem; and so on. Those avoided in this way always, in my experience, feel at least a little hurt. For Vicki it was an agonizing experience. She felt totally rejected.

It was a few weeks later that her pediatrician involved me.

"The prognosis is up in the air," he told me. "The child has visual problems. She's certainly delayed. I don't know about brain damage. She's almost seven months old and looks and acts like a newborn. I hope you can help her."

Vicki's home was a pleasant house in a new development, and most of the times I went there it was quite neat and clean. Though a good deal overweight, Vicki was pretty and seemed quite calm and easy-going until she picked up Amber. Then she became tense, holding the baby as if she were a cold, partially burned chunk of fireplace wood that would dirty with soot anything it touched.

Amber responded in kind. Almost every time Vicki picked her up she arched her back as if trying to escape and cried the newborn's shrill cry. I had an idea that I might be able to break up this destructive pattern, so I picked up Amber, ignored her reactions, cuddled her close, and chattered away.

"Now, Amber. This isn't the hospital. I'm not going to hurt you. You can scream all you like, but I won't stop cuddling. You're going to get used to it. You're going to love it."

In print this looks a bit simple-minded, but in practice I've found that it often works well for me just to go ahead and do what I want to persuade a mother like Vicki to do. And to some extent it worked this time. When I put Amber on a blanket on the floor and got down beside her, Vicki joined us and watched carefully while I put the baby through her paces.

She was much better off than I had thought she might be. Although far behind her chronological age level, she had good muscle tone and full range of motion at all her joints except for stiffness at her ankles where tubes had been inserted in her veins for long periods. I explained all this to Vicki as I went along and ended by suggesting that for a start she concentrate on helping and encouraging Amber to raise her head while lying on the floor both prone and supine. After I showed her a couple of times what I meant, Vicki was able to do it quite easily.

"Great," I told her. "You've got it just right."

For a few moments she knelt there and stared at the floor, saying nothing. I waited.

"How would you like it," she finally mumbled, "if your baby was blind."

She was playing the tragic queen, but I could not blame her.

"It would be terrible," I agreed. "But Amber isn't completely blind. There's no way to tell how much she's going to be able to see eventually. It could be quite a lot. And there are a lot of things you can do to help her make the most use of what sight she has. You can touch her more and move her around a lot and talk to her every chance you get. That way you will encourage her to move around a lot and take more interest in the world around her so she'll try harder to make sense of what she does see."

This seemed to make an impression on Vicki, so I got specific. I suggested that she plan four half-hour play periods a day for Amber, keep the light bright during them, and do everything she could think of to keep the baby stimulated and interested in what was going on around her. Maybe George could take charge of one of those play periods during the evening.

In the next few weeks the relationship between Vicki and Amber got distinctly more relaxed and hopeful. Vicki held the baby much more naturally, and Amber did not always seem to be trying to draw away from her. And once when I was there, with Amber on the floor supporting some of her weight on her forearms and holding up her head, I moved slowly from side to side in front of her. She turned her head to follow me with her eyes. Although Vicki was watching at the time, she didn't realize what Amber's movements meant, and I had to point out that she must be seeing me move.

"Oh, wow," said Vicki. "Am I ever dumb! But yeah, sure. She must be seeing you. Hey, that's terrific."

That was the day I met George, who came home earlier than usual. He seemed utterly colorless, as shy and dull as a human being can be. He showed not the faintest flicker of interest in either Vicki or Amber. I drove home sorrowing over what the fates had done and were doing to the three of them.

And yet for several months things were not so bad. Amber made many gains. She learned to roll over, to sit up with support, and to pick, hold, and throw toys. Prone on her chest she would "swim" with her head; legs, and arms off the floor and soon learned to get up on her hands and knees. And then one day she smiled at me. It was almost certain proof that she could see not just movement but also facial expressions. We are not born knowing how to smile but learn to do it by imitating the expressions we see on the faces of those around us, most often on the face of the mother.

Vicki was down on the floor with us the first time I saw Amber smile. She insisted she had never seen Amber do it before. Perhaps she simply hadn't noticed. But that was the high point of their relationship.

At that time Vicki would occasionally cuddle Amber with real warmth and talk to her. Now and then Amber would respond to her a little, but most of the time she remained extraordinarily irritable. Occasionally, she was crying inconsolably when I arrived. It could have been colic or teething or some sort of injury to her nervous system, of course. But it probably was not any of these.

One day when Amber was about a year old, I arrived at the house to find her strapped to an infant seat in the living room and screaming. Vicki was in the kitchen, drinking coffee and reading a magazine. I had to go around to the back door to get attention. And soon that became the way I found them most often.

Vicki didn't mind talking about this.

"I do what I can," she said. "You don't have to be here and listen to her all the time. Neither does George. Sometimes I have to put cotton in my ears and get in the shower and stay there till the hot water runs out just to get away from the noise she makes. I don't hate her or anything. I want to take care of her. Only not *all* the time, for god's sake."

To try to help her feel less isolated, I talked her into attending an evening meeting of parents of handicapped children. For many mothers it is a wonderful source of support and of

tips about how to deal with behavior problems. George stayed
with Amber, so it was an evening off for Vicki. But she never
opened her mouth at the meeting and never went to another
one.

Soon Amber began developing new tantrum devices—holding her breath, biting her hand, and voluntary vomiting. All
of them were unpleasant for anyone working with her. For
Vicki they were totally defeating.

One bleak, rainy winter afternoon I arrived to find Vicki
dry-eyed and exhausted. Amber was in her crib, screaming
and thrashing around. Vicki talked in a monotone.

"I can't do it any more. I'm too tired and I'm afraid I'll
hurt her. I hit her too hard. She doesn't know—I don't know
—I'm afraid I'll hurt her and I don't want to. I just can't do
it any more."

I called George and suggested that he get in touch with a
social worker who had been to see Vicki a couple of times.
When George got home, I dressed Amber and took her out
for a ride in my car. She soon calmed down, so I took her to a
supermarket, put her in a cart, and spent an hour wheeling
her around among all those delights. She was fascinated and
good as gold.

When we got back to her home, the social worker was
waiting for us. George had taken Vicki to their doctor. They
had decided to try to place Amber in a temporary foster home
to give Vicki a rest. She got it in a convalescent home for
patients suffering nervous breakdowns.

We struck it lucky in our choice of a foster home for Amber. Her foster mother is a warm, energetic woman with two
young children of her own and a loving, consistent way of
dealing with them which she easily transferred to Amber. The
baby's tantrums quickly tapered off and, within a week, ceased
altogether.

With her two-year-old foster brother as her model, she
soon learned to pull up to standing and cruise around from
one handhold to another. She also has begun babbling a lot,
calling her foster mother "ma-ma," her foster brother "ba-ba,"

and cake or anything else she likes to eat "kay." We still cannot be sure about how much vision she has, but she has developed a much greater range of facial expressions which she almost certainly has learned by observing and imitating the members of her foster family.

So how did it all happen? Why is Vicki such a failure as a mother?

I think several different layers of bad luck are wrapped around that failure. Vicki's own mother is one layer. I once tried to talk to the mother about Vicki's problems with Amber. The older woman's reaction amounted to not much more than a shrug.

George is another layer. Things would have been much different for Vicki if she had married a more giving sort of man. Her own childhood no doubt made it likely that she would tend to be more comfortable with a cool and distant man like George, but that did not make it inevitable that she should marry such a person.

Probably the worst luck of all was the condition in which Amber was born and her being snatched away so quickly and for so long. The term "maternal instinct" is badly misleading. It takes a lot of commitment to be a good mother. Some women find it easy to make that commitment quickly and totally. Others can make it only slowly and a little at a time. Vicki seems to be one of the latter. She needed encouragement. Instead, the medical procedure necessary to save Amber's life imposed on Vicki profound discouragement despite all the efforts to bring mother and child together as soon as possible.

How it will end remains, at this writing, to be seen. If Vicki recovers and Amber returns home less fearful and demanding, it is not inconceivable that Vicki will be able to start making the necessary commitment of herself to her role as mother. Or Vicki and George may decide to let Amber's foster parents adopt her, which the latter now would like to do.

I'm glad I do not have to decide which outcome will be the best for all concerned.

12

Single Father and Son:
A Handicapped but Loving Couple
An Infant with Delayed Gross Motor Skills

ALMOST ALWAYS the parent I work with is the mother, though some fathers do more than others to help with handicapped babies. In several cases the mothers I've worked with have been living alone with their children. Only in one case have I worked with a father living alone with his child. But it was a fascinating case.

A public health nurse—a friend I'll call Gail—got me involved. She saw an urgent need and skipped the usual channels.

"I've got a remarkable pair for you. One's an eight-month-old boy named Orion. Way behind in his development. He lives with his father who is recovering from an accident. They *both* need physical therapy."

She went on to explain that two months previously Sheila, Orion's mother, had walked out on him and his father, announcing that she was never coming back. A couple of weeks later the father—"officially named John but everyone calls him Ringo"—had lost the tips of three fingers of his left hand in an accident at the construction site where he worked. At the moment he was glum and overwhelmed by his own and his son's problems, but Gail felt that with a little help he could learn to cope and that both he and Orion would be better off if they stayed together.

I was feeling overloaded with work and would have had

little trouble resisting such an appeal to act without authorization had it come from almost anyone other than Gail. Most public health or, as they used to be called, visiting nurses tend to be of the get-involved persuasion, and Gail's involvement is total when someone really needs her help. Once, for instance, she found a new single mother deeply depressed and living in filth. She returned the next day, a Saturday, and spent it cleaning the apartment, organizing and stocking the kitchen cupboard and refrigerator, and preparing a meal for the mother and baby and herself. Her only explanation was— "I didn't have any special plans that day."

When I arrived unannounced at Ringo's tiny, telephoneless mobile home, his first reaction was hostile suspicion. He didn't want no do-gooder poking her nose in his business. My explanation of the infant program I worked in soothed him, though, and he let me come in and start getting acquainted with Orion.

He was very skinny for an eight-month-old, weighing barely thirteen pounds, and his cry sounded like that of a much younger child. But he took a lot of interest in what was going on around him and had a sweet smile and a coy way of peering up at me through his long, thick lashes. It was easy to win his trust and attention by playing peek-a-boo and tickling him gently.

I persuaded Ringo to spread a blanket on the floor and put Orion on it face down so that I could see how he rolled over, turned, and reached for things that interested him. He simply didn't. After whimpering a little, he raised his head, pushed up a bit on his arms, looked around, then slowly collapsed back down to the floor. I put a musical toy a little way in front of him and made it play. This brought his head up again, and he tried to reach toward the toy. But the reach amounted to little more than a vague wave.

"He seems tired," I said.

"Yeah," said Ringo. "He probably is. We were out late last night."

I started to protest about a baby's need for undisturbed rest but checked myself in time. Clearly, he was trying to get a rise out of me. So instead of rising I concentrated on trying to work out Orion's developmental level. Since he could roll over, though just barely, had weak trunk muscles, and was able to support his head for only short stretches, I decided that he was operating at about the level of a three- to four-month-old. I felt sure that I could help but only, of course, if Ringo wanted my help. I asked whether there was anything about Orion's behavior or appearance that especially concerned him.

"Well, I don't know much about kids . . . I wish he'd eat right, though."

What was wrong with the way he ate?

"He let's the milk run out of his mouth a lot. We're both covered all over with milk by the time he finishes a bottle."

Would he show me?

He got the bottle, picked up Orion, laid him face up across his lap, and put the nipple in the baby's mouth. Orion was almost horizontal and the bottle nearly vertical, so a stream of milk ran from each corner of his mouth. He didn't even put his hands on the bottle.

I rearranged the baby with his head up in the crook of his father's left arm and supported on one side by his father's chest. Then I put Orion's hands around his bottle. His expression changed from one of resigned misery to a glow of hungry interest. He grasped the bottle firmly, closed his mouth tightly around the nipple, and sucked hard.

"Hey," said Ringo. "Wow. Ain't no milk spilling out at all. I guess you really know how."

My first reaction was, I must admit, plain sexist. No woman, I felt sure, would ever have tried to feed a baby Ringo's way. How could a man be so dumb as not to realize that the result of his procedure was inevitable?

But I got over that fairly fast. It was clear that Ringo loved his son and wanted to do well by him. Although he and

Orion's mother had not been legally married, her abrupt departure had been for him a severe emotional wrench. The accident to his hand also had been more than just physically painful. Considering what he had been through, he probably was doing as well by Orion as could be expected. He certainly was trying hard.

I asked about his hand and said I might be able to give him a little help with it. He told me that a rickety power saw had fallen apart while he was using it, and the blade had severed the middle, ring, and little fingers of his left hand down to the knuckles. By the time I saw them, though, the knuckles were healing very nicely. I told him so and said he must have had an unusually good surgeon because it was going to be a very neat looking hand.

"Yeah?" he said, astonished.

"See how smooth the scars are? They'll fade until they won't be noticeable at all. And you've still got your thumb and forefinger. Those are the most important parts of a hand."

"No kidding? My friends all say it looks cruddy."

"That's just because they saw the hand in bandages and heard all about the accident. And when the bandages first came off, the scars would have been red and mean looking. New people you meet won't notice. I once knew a guy who had lost a couple of fingers several years before I met him. I didn't even notice they were missing until I'd known him for months."

"Hey. Wow. That's really something."

"How do you feel now?"

"Well, if I bump one of them, it sure hurts. But most of the time, nothing. Except my wrist is kind of sore."

I checked the range of motion in his arm, wrist, and hand. All were a little tight, probably as a result of weeks in a sling plus the pain and fear he had been through. I showed him some simple exercises to help loosen them and made a few suggestions. For instance, washing dishes, clothes, and Orion in warm water would be good for the hand and remaining fingers. He was delighted with the attention and reassurances, so I switched the subject back to Orion.

"He's a long way behind in his development," I explained. "By now he ought to be able to sit up by himself and roll over and crawl around. It would be a good idea to have a baby specialist look him over."

That opened the floodgates. Ringo wasn't about to have no damn specialist messing around any more with his kid. It was because of one of them that Orion's mother, Sheila, had deserted them. When Orion was about five months old, a series of ear infections and other problems had led them to take him to a hospital where they had kept him for a week. The day they took him home some doctor told them that he might end up partially deaf. For some reason this terrified Sheila. She told Ringo she couldn't take it, went away for a few days, returned for a week, then left for good.

"And he can hear and see as good as you and me," Ringo wound up. "That was some specialist."

I could detect nothing wrong with Orion's sight or hearing, and neither, it turned out later, could anyone else. Probably the man who had seen him in the hospital had had some ill-thought-out idea of "preparing the parents for the worst" that could result from the infections. After a lot of telling and retelling of his sad story, Ringo calmed to the point of being able to understand that it was I who had to have Orion checked by a pediatrician in order to be authorized to work with him. Eventually, one of the best in the community made a thorough examination and found nothing wrong with his sight, hearing, or any other specific functions. The verdict was that Orion was slow in his development for unknown, undetectable reasons, and the kind of help I could provide might make a great deal of difference in the way he grew up.

In the course of helping Ringo fill out the inevitable forms I discovered that he was close to flat broke. He had innocently allowed himself to be hustled into accepting a small lump sum for his lost fingers and had signed agreements ending any hope of getting more. I told him that he and Orion together would qualify for various kinds of state aid, food stamps, and such.

"You mean welfare?" was his reaction. "I don't know—I don't think—I don't want to—I don't want that kind of help."

A lot of people seem to think that this reaction is now extremely rare. In the years since I went back to practicing my profession, I have worked with seventeen families who have been "on welfare." Only three of the seventeen failed to make frequent, strenuous, and sooner or later successful efforts to break away from their dependence on such help, and those three were so deeply mired in trouble that they had no energy left over from merely and barely surviving.

By stressing Orion's needs I persuaded Ringo to talk to a social worker about temporary help until he was able to go back to work. Then Gail and I got together and worked out a program for teaching Ringo the elements of baby care in tactful ways he could accept. And at last I was able to get down to work with Orion.

Since his limpness and inertness did not result from any detectable disability, physical or mental, it seemed to me that the thing to do was challenge him over and over to try to do what he should be doing. I taught Ringo how to help him roll over, then try to get him to do it by himself, and the same with sitting up and kneeling on all fours. When I returned a week later, Ringo already had gotten great results. As I might have expected, however, the results had nothing to do with rolling over, sitting, or kneeling. Ringo assured me that he had spent an hour or more every day of the week doing the sort of thing I had taught him to. Orion still could not or would not do any of them by himself, but when I arrived he was doing what seemed to be push-ups and, in between pushes, kicking out with his feet. There was nothing to do but laugh.

"Now you see," I told Ringo, "how we experts work, our wonders to perform. If I had tried to get him to do push-ups, he'd probably be rolling over, sitting up, and crawling all around the place."

It is conceivable, of course, that Orion's trouble was some sort of more or less temporary neurological cross-wiring. That is only speculation, but he did in several ways react unexpectedly, put the cart before the horse, and so on. The important thing, however, was that he did act and react, starting the necessary exploring and testing of his own body and reflexes.

In the process he put his father through a crash course in the rewards and tribulations of parenthood. On the occasion of the push-ups Ringo was full of enthusiasm about the good side.

"I never thought much about having kids," he told me. "He was an accident, but I'm sure glad he's here now. I really dig the way he's thrashing around on the floor like that and it's great seeing him asleep in his bed and the way he reaches up to me when he wakes up."

I loaned him a couple of books about how children grow and the kinds of things parents can do to encourage and reward them. For three weeks Ringo's enthusiasm stayed high, and Orion seemed to get steadily more and more active. But unless Ringo or I propped him up, his activities all were of the kind he could perform while lying on his back or stomach. So one day I found Ringo with the tribulations uppermost.

"Maybe I shouldn't be trying to do this. Maybe I can't . . . It's hard to be alone. Sometimes I think he'd be better off if he was . . . if someone else took care of him."

Most parents, and especially single parents, feel that way once in a while if they are honest with themselves. Parents of handicapped children obviously have even more reason for occasional periods of depression. But for Ringo such periods never have lasted long.

This is partly because Orion has made good and quite noticeable progress from time to time, though often in unexpected and out-of-the-ordinary ways. He is distinctly and inexplicably delayed in what are sometimes called "the gross motor skills" such as sitting up independently and crawling on all fours. But in some of the "fine motor skills" he has been almost precocious.

Once, for instance, I propped him up amid some pillows, with Ringo standing by to help if he started tipping over, and got him interested in trying to put little plastic doughnuts on a post with a rocker base. The idea was to get him to figure out how to manage the post's unsteadiness. He met the challenge in a way I've never seen used by any other child so young (he was only a year old at the time). He maneuvered the doughnuts one at a time with both hands and steadied the rocking post with his feet.

Another time I gave him two wooden blocks. When he was holding one in each hand, I presented a third to him. He put the one in his right hand between his feet, grasping it with his toes, and reached for the third.

Many babies sit up by themselves by the age of six months and most do so by seven or eight months. At twelve months Orion still would not get into the position by himself, nor hold it when placed in it unless supported in some way. Yet one day when I arrived on my weekly visit, Ringo went to fetch him from his crib and excitedly called me to come see. And there was Orion standing. He was holding hard onto the railing, of course, but he was standing all by himself. I have never heard or read of another child who learned to stand before sitting nor have I been able to make a guess why it should have happened that way with Orion.

He also was a little, though not much, delayed in developing his use of language. Most ten-month-olds, for instance, apply "mama" and "dada" to the appropriate person and regularly use another word or two with clearly understandable intent. Orion was a couple of months past his first birthday before he began calling Ringo "dada." But with his usual atypicality he had distinctly more than average enthusiasm for unintelligible babbling.

It was also at about fourteen months that he at last began getting into and briefly holding the sitting position all by himself, though he would sooner or later—and usually sooner—topple over backwards. By then he was quite nonchalant about pulling himself to standing and cruising around while holding onto chairs, people, or other objects. His progress helped give Ringo the confidence to start putting his life back together.

His hand was well healed, and he was able to piece out his welfare payments with earnings from carpentry repairs, yard work, and other odd jobs. One of my single mothers told me about a single parent group sponsored by a church, and I passed the word on to Ringo. He found several new friends, including another father-son combination, and one of the mothers in the group was glad to have Orion spend part of the day at her place in exchange for Ringo's doing household repairs. This gave him a chance to sign up for a rehabilitation training program that eventually helped him get a job in the city parks department.

But Orion remained the center of his life. I continued to see them once a week, and I know that Ringo spent many hours a day wheedling his son through the exercises I suggested. These stayed focused on his walking and sitting problems.

For a long time his walking stuck at the cruising stage, though he did get better and better at it. But if you led him by the hand away from any possible support and let go, he simply sat down and soon toppled over onto his back. He was good-natured about it and not at all anxious or defiant. He just could not or would not walk by himself.

At fifteen months he would sometimes get up to a sitting position all by himself and hold it, his back straight, for ten minutes or so. Then he would suddenly topple over backwards. It was as if he abruptly forgot how to maintain his balance.

So Ringo and I worked at getting him to practice skills that seemed likely to be helpful. I got an inflated pillow, put it on the floor with Orion on it, then slowly moved it in various ways. In no time at all he was able to keep his balance when we moved the pillow sideways or backward, but the instant it moved forward he would start to topple over backward, though our stopping the movement and a little very gentle support at his shoulder would stop the topple.

Walking exercises included getting him to walk sideways; to stand for a while first on one foot, then the other; to hold onto his support with only one hand and manipulate something with the other; to lean against the support with his chest and manipulate something with both hands; and to bend over and pick up toys with one hand while holding onto the support with the other hand. We must have put him through these and similar routines hundreds of times. I have to think that they helped, but for months there was little indication that they were doing so.

Yet his progress in many fine motor skills was rapid. The daughter of the woman with whom he spent his days was a few months older than he, and he had to watch her eat just once to learn to handle a spoon for himself with elegant aplomb. He also took up chattering with or at her in what sounded remarkably like sentences.

Eventually, in spite of the thorough examination he had been given when I started working with him and regular checkups by the pediatrician, I began to be uneasy about his walking and sitting difficulties. He might have some subtle neurological problem that needed treatment. Perhaps he ought to go to one of the big urban hospitals to be seen by a variety of specialists. I thought it likely that Ringo would resist the suggestion, so I started building up to it in a roundabout way.

Orion took the matter out of my hands. By about a month before his second birthday he was able to walk quite confidently holding onto no more than a short length of garden hose held at the other end by someone he trusted. Walking across the room this way with me on the other end of the hose, he let go of it to brush a fly away from his face and took a few steps by himself before casually grasping the hose again. A week later he got up from sitting and walked across the room by himself to investigate my bag of toys. And never since has he had any noticeable trouble in either walking or sitting.

At this writing he has needed no help from me for more than two years and is going to nursery school. Ringo has a new live-in girlfriend who seems fond of Orion, and all goes well as far as I can tell. It is possible, of course, that at some later age other problems will show up in Orion's life, but as of now all that can be said about him is that he was atypical in the way he learned to move around.

13

"Mama, car"

A Child with Brain Damage

RINGING THE BELL I admired the magnificent double doors of carved oak, the stained glass windows alongside them, and the really stunning view down the valley. It was the largest and most expensive house I had ever visited. Disaster does not spare the rich.

Because there are no physical therapists in private practice working with handicapped infants in our area, the agency with which I work does not inquire about the income of a family with an infant for whom a pediatrician asks help. A social worker had told me that this family was very wealthy, indeed, with inherited money and no regular employment for any family member. But that was strictly private information and had no pertinence to my work.

What was pertinent was the information given me concerning the family's only son, two-year-old Derek. Several weeks earlier he had gone for a ride into town with his mother and had been standing on the back seat of the family Bentley when a drunken boy in a huge pickup truck ran a red light and plowed into the side of the car. Derek's mother had been only slightly injured. Derek has suffered fractures of one arm, one leg, and his skull, many bad bruises, and internal injuries. He had been in a coma for a week but then had recovered enough to take liquid from a bottle and semi-solid food from a spoon. The skull fracture was healed and the others healing well, but he had not yet made any further recovery.

His mother, Tracey, answered the door and led me into an

enormous living room with what looked to me like original old masters on the walls, many fresh-cut flowers in bouquets, and trees in tubs in the corners. I asked about Derek.

"Oh, he's much better," she said.

She stopped, gulped, and looked down at her hands in her lap.

"I keep telling people he's better," she half sobbed. "And at first he was, he was. But now I don't know. He was hurt very, very badly."

She stopped and sobbed openly. But very quietly.

"I've been told he is eating and swallowing," I said when she had calmed down a bit. "That certainly means progress. It takes coordination which is a very good sign after such an accident. It means something is healing in his brain. So you're right. He is better."

"If only you had seen him before. . . . He was running and climbing and talking a blue streak. He'd climb on his rocking horse and bounce and squeal. . . . Now he just lies there and whines most of the time he's awake. Sometimes I pick him up and rock with him in the rocking chair. Do you think that's all right? He usually stops whining when I do it."

I assured her that cuddling was excellent therapy and asked about her own injuries. The only physical problems she had left, she said, were a few aches and bruises of no importance, but she was seeing a psychotherapist. She knew the accident was not her fault but was still having a hard time with her feeling of guilt about not forcing Derek to sit beside her and use the safety harness which he had resisted as vehemently as only a two-year-old can.

"You just can't let a two-year-old make decisions like that," she told me. "I'm always going to feel guilty about it. I have to learn to live with the feeling."

I admired her courage and the skill of the therapist who was helping her confront all this head-on. Her husband, she told me, had always left Derek entirely to her, and she wanted all the responsibility, now more than ever. She could not bear to turn any of it over to a nurse or nanny, though she did have two nurse's aides who took turns coming in most afternoons and evenings to give her some respite. There were also, I later learned, a cook, a maid, and a gardener, all living in.

Derek's room on the second floor was huge and better stocked than our local toy library. Large, stuffed airplanes and rocket ships made of brightly colored fabrics hung from the beamed ceiling, and the crib was surrounded with stuffed animals, enormous fire trucks, and such. But the only thing in the crib with him was a faded blanket tucked under his cheek.

"His security blanket," Tracey told me. "He used to drag it around with him, just like Linus in the *Peanuts* cartoons. I really think he rests better when he has it there with him."

If true, this was good news, and it was not impossible that, knowing him so well, she could really tell when he was resting better. His two years of healthy growth and development certainly made his prospects brighter than those for a child who suffers brain damage at or near birth. What he had already learned had created many neural pathways and patterns, and at least some of them could in all probability be challenged back into effectiveness.

It was very difficult to lift him out of the crib, totally inert as he was, because of the weight of his arm and leg cast. I said so and Tracey heartily agreed. I suggested putting a regular bed in his room until he became more active.

"How about a water bed?" she asked. "We have a few in various guest rooms."

I couldn't help remembering Scott Fitzgerald's famous remark about the very rich being different from the rest of us. I assured her it was a great idea, at least for the daytime, since it would give him feedback whenever he moved, and suggested that she have the water bed set up along with an ordinary bed for his night's sleep.

We put Derek, who had been asleep and started whining when we waked him, on a mattress on the floor. Experimentally, I tried stroking his face, arms, hands, and tummy, all the while talking to him in a low, gentle tone. The whine ceased abruptly. Another hopeful sign.

That was the last bit of hope I could find on my first visit, but it amounted to more than it sounds like. It meant that he could respond to some stimuli. And that in turn meant that it would be very much worthwhile to keep providing him a wide variety of stimuli in attempts to arouse his interest in seeing, hearing, touching, tasting, and smelling things and moving whatever parts of himself he could relearn how to move.

I explained this at length to Tracey and gave her a long list of suggestions with demonstrations of how to put them into practice. Suggestions about keeping boldly marked and brightly colored things about him in bed and dangling them before his eyes whenever he opened them. Suggestions about toys that would make pleasant noises whenever he chanced to touch them and about talking or reading to him and playing records, even if he did not seem to notice. Suggestions about touching and stroking different parts of his bare skin with her hands and soft cloths. Suggestions about occasionally spraying a little perfume in the air near him or burning a little incense. And suggestions about feeding him not standard baby food but little bits of whatever had been his favorite table foods before the accident.

She made notes on all this with great interest and in great detail. In connection with my last suggestion she made Fitzgerald seem somewhat less fatuous: Two of Derek's favorite foods, it seemed, had been onion soup and Brie. I like them, too, but did not acquire the tastes until I was about thirty and have a twenty-year-old son who still considers them inedible. Ah, well.

She thanked me heartily and wanted to know what time I could come back the next day. Fearful that money might be about to be waved under my nose, I explained gently but firmly that my visits would be limited to one a week and that there would be no point in making them more frequent. My role was to show her what to do and to help her assess results at regular intervals. I would be glad to have her call me at home if she had any problems or if any exciting new improvement came along. She took it well and never again tried to claim any extra share of my time.

On my next visit I found that, much as expected, she was following almost all my suggestions but in some cases much too tentatively out of fear of hurting him. She had been getting a few small results, too; he was blinking his eyes or turning his head toward something that seemed to interest him. She seemed just a little tired and discouraged, though.

Had Derek before the accident liked being tickled, I asked. He had loved it, but now he didn't respond at all, she told me.

I kneeled over him where he lay on a mattress on the floor, sang him a little song I had sung my own children at his age, and tickled vigorously under his arms and down along his rib cage. He blinked rapidly, broke into a brief but wide grin, and emitted what sounded like a cross between a snort and a grunt, but definitely a happy snort-grunt.

"Oh, oh," Tracey gasped. "His first smile!"

I picked him up and handed him to her. She hugged him and cried. I cried, too. Then we wiped our eyes, blew our noses, and put on a record for Derek while we had some tea and I told her about experiences of mine with other children who resembled Derek in this way or that.

After that it was easy to persuade her to be more vigorous in her efforts with him. I showed her how to rub his hands over his favorite toys, tell him their names, bring them to his mouth for taste tests, and move his arms in appropriate gestures while he held them, such as shaking a rattle. I also suggested that she not keep him in his room all the time but move him now and then to other parts of the house for at least brief stays.

By my third visit his arm and leg casts had been removed.

The sight of his atrophied limbs was sad even for me, though not nearly so much as for Tracey. She cried through most of that session but never once tried to turn away.

A newborn baby usually and gradually gets control first of its head, then of its trunk, then of its arms and legs, and I suggested that we try in general, though not too rigidly, to bring Derek along in that order. He did seem to relearn that way over the next couple of months, though no one could possibly say how much it was because we expected him to and urged him that way and how much it was his natural order of recovery.

Typical was the way he learned to feed himself again. I showed Tracey how to prop him up in his high chair, wrap his fingers around finger food or a cup of some liquid, and convey it to his mouth. She had been doing this now and then for only three days when, having turned her back on him in his high chair for a moment, she turned back to see him lift a cookie to his mouth and shove it in.

About a week after that, she called me one evening in great excitement. Again, he had been propped in his high chair, and this time she had stepped out of the room for a moment. When she returned, he had slumped over sideways and was unable to right himself. He was calling for help.

"I don't really know whether he was saying 'mama' or just 'ma.' He said it over and over. It *is* a great day, isn't it?"

It was, indeed. And as a result of Tracey's dedication and long hours of work with Derek, it was followed by many more great days. One was the day he first rolled over from his back onto his front, then lifted his head and grinned at her. Another was when he first sat up without support. Another was when he began babbling; the sounds were just vowels laced with an occasional consonant at first, but they were full of promise. And then there was the day we put him on his rocking horse and he was able, with minimal support from me, to make it move a little. He laughed a wonderful, gleeful laugh.

At this writing he is about to turn three. He is much

better than the inert lump he was when he came home from the hospital after the accident. Now, for instance, he can get from his tummy to all fours, and then, using a chair or your leg, pull on up to standing. That's great. But. But it takes him about forty-five seconds, and that is three times as long as it took a fifteen-month-old I once timed. She was not a world champion type of fifteen-month-old, either.

Tracey's best friend gave birth to a daughter just a few weeks before Derek was born. When Tracey told me that she had been invited to bring Derek to the party for the girl's third birthday, I encouraged her to go but warned her about what to expect. In spite of my warning she was depressed by the experience. Her friend's daughter is a charmer who talks in complete sentences, operates a simple electronic game, is toilet trained, and rides a tricycle, sometimes on two wheels.

To help Tracey get over this I took her to a preschool for physically handicapped children. There were a few children noticeably worse off than Derek and others in somewhat better shape. Now she plans eventually to enroll him there for at least a year or two of day school because he will have the help both of a physical therapist and of a teacher especially trained to work with children like this.

I feel sure he is going to make a good deal more progress. In vocabulary, for instance, he already is well ahead of his stage of physical rehabilitation. He has one hundred words or more and seems to add new ones almost every day, which would be pretty good for a two-year-old.

He uses almost all of them singly but has begun to try combining two now and then. The first time Tracey heard him do this, his choice of the two words to combine was, from her point of view, overwhelmingly sad: "Mama, car."

Her face crumpled when she told me about it. She did not fantasize that he "meant something" by this. She knew the choice was accidental, apparently made because she had just come home and he had been looking out the window when she emerged from the car. But that didn't help much.

She is doing everything I know of that she can to atone for her mistake. It remains possible that eventually she will be able to help Derek wipe out all its ill effects. Although he still has a long way to go to full recovery, he has made enormous progress, and I know of no reason to set limits on how much further he can go.

14

Frighteningly Fragile

An Infant with Brittle Bones
and Slow Development

Margot was born a full-term, healthy baby—so far as anyone could tell. Her parents, Erica and Bob, were experienced in the role, having raised their first daughter, Hilary, for two years. They had planned Margot's birth for the beginning of Bob's summer vacation from his teaching job, because he wanted to do a lot of helping during Margot's first months. Money was plentiful, Erica bringing in a good share from her work as a free-lance window dresser for several shops and by selling the dried flower arrangements she makes to boutiques around the area.

In other words, it was a baby and family with just about everything going for them and no reason to anticipate any sort of problem. And when it showed up eight hours after Margot's birth, her problem did not seem like much. One of the nursery nurses detected slightly labored breathing. She checked with a stethoscope and found the chest sounds a little odd. Margot's body temperature proved to be up about two degrees.

That was sufficient reason to summon a physician. He diagnosed a mild pneumonia and ordered the appropriate antibiotic administered intravenously. Since newborns can dehydrate very quickly, he also ordered that supplemental liquids be given, too. All very right and proper and still no real cause for alarm.

"At that point," Erica later told me, "I thought it would be a story to tell Margot someday. About how she was so hoity-toity that she couldn't be bothered with a mere cold or runny nose and insisted from the beginning that, if she was going to have anything, it had to be at least pneumonia. Who worries about pneumonia? Everyone knows that antibiotics knock it out right away. Or so I thought."

By the end of her first twenty-four hours, however, Margot's temperature was 102°, and she had to be put in an oxygen tent. A culture was done on mucus from her throat. The bacteria causing her problem proved to be of a kind highly resistant to antibiotics.

More I.V. tubes, more antibiotics, more oxygen, and a lot more anxiety for Erica and Bob and their pediatrician. By the time Margot was two days old, she had to work hard to breathe even in an oxygen tent. Specialists made the decision to send her by plane to the nearest large medical center with an intensive care unit for newborn babies. A neonatal team consisting of a doctor and two nurses very considerately wheeled her in a special traveling incubator down to her mother's room to say goodbye.

"We'll call you as soon as we get there and she's tucked into her new bed. Try not to worry. The trip will only take two or three hours."

Even so, Erica told me, it was terrifying to see Margot in "that big tin can with tubes sticking out of her and three attendants all headed off into the night in a small plane."

"She'll be cold," Erica remembers telling them. "You don't have a blanket."

"Her bed is warmed and enclosed," the doctor explained. "She doesn't need a blanket."

Still on Erica's bed in its box was a baby blanket brought that day by a friend. Erica urged them to take it, "just in case." One of the nurses spread it over the plastic lid of the incubator and promised, "We'll take good care of her." And they were gone.

Four hours later the nurse called to say that Margot was all settled in, that a new antibiotic had been started, and that her blanket was rolled up with her in the incubator.

"We've taken a picture for you. And we can invite you to come up as soon as you can make the trip. There are rooms for parents right on the hospital grounds."

But the next day Margot's temperature went up to 104°, and she had several convulsions, a common result of prolonged high temperature. Antiseizure medication was added to all the rest she was receiving. By the time her parents got to the hospital, she was five days old and showing the effects of her battle to survive. Her breathing was fast and shallow. She had lost almost two pounds. Her X-rays showed larger areas of infection in her lungs. Her temperature was 105°.

"Things are not good," the specialist in charge told them. "She's using most of her energy just to breathe, so we want to put her on a respirator that will breathe for her. We also need to do a simple procedure under local anesthesia. It's so that we can suction out some of the gunk accumulating in her breathing tubes."

He gently described the tracheotomy procedure. A surgeon would make a small incision in the baby's throat and on through into her trachea, then insert a tube for cleaning but also to provide a way of channeling oxygen directly into the lungs. The hole and tube would be small but noticeable, and temporary. When the tube could be removed and the incision permitted to heal, only a tiny scar would be left.

Erica and Bob agreed to the procedure. Unluckily, no one thought to tell them that Margot would be unable to make any sounds unless the opening was held closed. When she gained enough strength to cry a few days later, the lack of sound was a nasty shock for Erica.

"I could see that she was crying," she told me. "But there wasn't a whisper of sound. I had the horrible thought that my real baby was dead and this was just a puppet. It was all those tubes that made it look as if it were alive. I felt half dead myself."

But this was only a passing phase for Erica, even though

the prospects for Margot kept getting worse. For one thing, she needed increasingly greater percentages of oxygen, and it had to be forced into her lungs under greater pressure. The staff warned that, for a certain small proportion of the children who need it, such a level of oxygen results in damage to the retina. Unlike the parents of Amber, the premature baby who also needed oxygen (as I described in an earlier chapter), Erica and Bob were able to understand and accept the risk. They were assured that the oxygen was essential to keep Margot alive, that it was being carefully monitored, and that it would be tapered off as soon as she could get along with less of it.

The tapering off came about with agonizing slowness and tentativeness, though the infection yielded fairly suddenly. One morning her temperature was 103°, by that evening it was 100°, and two days later it reached and stayed close to normal. X-rays showed her lungs cleared. Yet every time the respirator was turned off, she would seem all right for two or three minutes, then gradually begin breathing faster and faster and with more effort. She would start looking dusky around the mouth, and her fingers and toes would turn a bluish color.

It took a month to wean her from the respirator. During that month she at last began eating so that the sustaining I.V. tubes could be removed, too. She still had to stay under a hood where the atmosphere's usual 20 percent oxygen content could be raised to 40 percent, but it was at last conceivable that Erica and Bob could take care of her at home.

In preparation for the great move, the hospital gave Margot a thorough checkup, and suddenly there was great, good news. Her retinas had come through unharmed. There was no reason to expect her vision to be in any way impaired.

That was the last bit of good news for many months. Erica and Bob were taught how to take care of Margot's trachea tube, how to suction mucus from her trachea with a miniature vacuum cleaner, how to set up the hood, and how to keep the oxygen level under it close to 40 percent. They took her home and three days later had to rush her back to the intensive care unit with "an upper respiratory infection"—that is, a cold. What would be a mere nuisance for most babies was a dire threat to Margot's life.

And so it went through the first eight months of her life. She would get settled at home for a few days or a couple of weeks, then have to be rushed off in sudden danger of asphyxiation. The only improvements during this time were that she became able to spend her waking hours outside the hood and that the local hospital acquired equipment with which to help her, so that she did not always have to go all the way back to the medical center when she caught a bug.

Eventually, the specialists who studied her worked out a three-way explanation of her problem. She probably had been born with smaller than average lung capacity, as of course are many of us. The pneumonia infection probably had destroyed some of her lung tissue, the cells that absorb oxygen from air and transmit it to red blood cells for distribution throughout the body. And the high pressure oxygen necessary to save her life inevitably had destroyed a little more tissue. Since nothing could be done about any of these factors, this was not a great deal of help, but it did indicate that she probably would not get worse.

When I first saw her at the end of her first eight months, she was the most frighteningly fragile baby I had ever dealt with. At that age most babies are roly-poly and smiling. They crawl everywhere, sit up by themselves, and fling toys about. Margot was scrawny, expressionless, and inert except when cringing from strangers. Her pediatrician warned me that her bones were thin and probably brittle, so that sudden movements could cause fractures—a possibility that almost paralyzes a physical therapist. Even Erica still was a little afraid of her and carried her about on a pillow.

All Margot's unavoidable but horrendous hospital experiences had made the sight of a stranger a cause for terror. Her soundless crying and pulling back when I came in view made me pull back in turn. I was afraid not only of hurting her and making her more miserable. I also doubted that I would be able to do anything to help her.

I calmed myself and suggested to Erica that she sit at one end of the couch with Margot on the pillow on her lap and that I sit at the other end where Margot could see me and perhaps get used to the sight. We talked for an hour and a half, and the baby did get to the stage of looking at me without shrinking. Erica let herself go to within hailing distance of hysteria, switching repeatedly from crying to laughing and back again.

Actually, she had learned to cope with great success. Hilary, she told me, was almost three and intensely resentful of the chaos Margot had brought into her life. "I hate Margot" was one of her lines and "Take her back to the hozzibal" another. Erica wisely ignored such remarks and spent as much time as she could reading to Hilary, taking her for walks, and visiting her preschool classes. Bob did what he could to free her for such times, though he was still squeamish about using the suction machine and handling the trachea tube. But they had managed to hire a nurse to come in for several hours twice a week and give Erica some real time off.

On my second visit I was inspired to try standing behind Erica and, over her shoulder, to play peek-a-boo with Margot. Erica said no one had tried it before. The first couple of times I popped up over her mother's head Margot showed surprise and interest instead of fear. Then I popped out sideways. She blinked—and ever so faintly she smiled. It was a triumph. But it didn't last. When I sat down beside Erica, Margot shrank away and went into her usual silent crying jag.

"Oh, Margot," Erica sighed. "What am I going to do with you?"

"You give her a good talking to this week," I said as I gathered up my useless toys.

The third visit was a repeat but, when I arrived for the fourth, Erica was looking determined.

"Margot's nine months old and calling all the shots here," she told me. "It's not right. You just go ahead and barge in. If she cries herself into a fit, we'll give her oxygen. I think it's more important that she gets moving than that she should feel safe all the time."

That put the burden on me and reinvigorated my fears about those brittle bones, so I was very, very tentative. My best move that day was reversing roles with Erica, holding Margot on her pillow on my lap and having her mother do the peek-a-boos. She cried at first, as expected, but gave it up when it didn't work by getting rid of me. A couple of times she smiled broadly at Erica's peeks and even waved her arms a bit.

I showed Erica how to stimulate her gently by rubbing her skin in different places several times a day with soft cloths. And I rearranged my schedule so that I could visit her twice a week for a while. My invasion of Margot's tiny world had to be very, very tentative, so it was important to keep and exploit any small advantages I gained. Also, Erica felt sure that Margot had really gotten much tougher than she seemed.

"And anyway," she said, "what kind of life will she have if we let her go on getting away with being afraid of everyone and everything?"

The decision made a big difference because it emboldened us. On my next visit Erica had the news that, for the first time, Margot had spent the entire previous night outside her oxygen hood with her mother and father taking turns sitting up to make sure all went well. I decided on the spot to celebrate by giving the baby another new experience. I spread a towel on the floor, had Erica place Margot on her back in the middle of it, then we each picked up two corners of the towel and gently swung her back and forth while singing "Rock-a-bye-baby." Margot looked utterly astounded and forgot to cry.

By then she was used to me and had not only stopped crying at the sight of me but would reach out for the toys I dangled before her. So I tried putting her on a soft blanket on a big bed and having Erica lift one side of the blanket just a little to give her the idea of rolling over toward the toys I dangled just out of her reach on the other side. When she started to cry, I sang "Rock-a-bye-baby." She stopped crying and gave me a puzzled look.

The next day she developed another cold and had to go back to our local hospital for three days, but this cost her none of her gains. She still recognized me even although she didn't see me for more than a week, and seemed almost eager to play my games. When another cold came along within a week of her return home, the pediatrician suggested that her parents try treating her at home. All they had to do for her was put her under the oxygen hood each night, let her use a little oxygen mask when she needed it during the day, and suction her trachea tube quite frequently.

"She really got over it all by herself," Erica crowed to me.

By then she had rolled over onto her stomach all by herself several times, but she seemed to hate that position. I brought along a wedge of foam rubber to support her trunk while her head and shoulders hung over the edge. She could support some of her weight on her arms but had to lift her head to see anything interesting. My usual toys soon bored her in this position, but a pan full of water with pingpong balls and rubber boats floating on it proved fascinating. She quickly learned to lean on one arm and splash in the water with the other.

By her first birthday life was beginning to have hopeful possibilities for her. She was no longer terrified of all strangers, sometimes even smiled at those who smiled at her. She was eating well and gaining weight rapidly. And she was making a lot of experiments.

What made most of them possible was that, although her gross motor skills were still developing slowly, she was zooming ahead with the fine ones. Her trachea tube may actually have helped stimulate this. First she learned that by forcing a lot of air past her vocal cords she could make faintly audible sounds. Then, possibly quite by accident, she discovered that by closing the trachea tube with her finger she could turn the faint sound into a howl. It probably would have been wonderful to see her face the first time this happened. At about the same time she startled Erica by taking out the removable, inner part of the tube and handing it over for cleaning.

Books were another great stimulus for her. By the age of fifteen months she was very fond of turning the pages of picture books, the kind with stiff pages that turn easily. One afternoon she was sitting on my lap with such a book when Erica started telling me something or other. For a few moments we ignored Margot, though I could feel that she was getting a bit restless. Finally, I looked down, while Erica went on talking, and saw that Margot was pointing at a picture and pushing the book toward her mother, who continued to ignore her. Margot stiffened and, in a decidedly forceful whisper, said: "Mama!"

Erica and I were astounded, of course. I think Margot was a little surprised, herself.

"What is it?" Erica asked, for lack of anything better to say.

Margot thumped the picture. "More!" she whispered. It was a picture of a glass of milk.

Service was fast. While she drank her milk, Erica and I talked in hushed voices about this unexpected development and about what her being able to speak would mean for her and for our work with her and for the rest of her family. By the next time I saw her, she had learned that by putting her finger over the trachea tube opening she could turn the whisper into a loud rasp. And she soon was rasping a blue streak —pointing at things or pictures in books and naming them or demanding food, toys, and wawa, her term for the pan of water with objects floating in it and intended, in her opinion, to be splashed out of it. She talked to herself while playing and soon began putting two words together into mini-sentences.

She began progressing fast in gross motor skills, too. She

still crept everywhere but could pull herself to standing in her crib or at a chair. When she did it, though, she always yelled for help to get back down, so I went to work to give her more confidence. I knelt behind her with my lap only a few inches from her bottom while she held herself standing by a chair, held her around the middle with one hand and pried her fingers loose with the other, saying "Sit, Margot." Scared at first, she was able in one session to graduate from dropping into my lap to dropping onto a fat pillow, then onto a thin pillow, and finally to the thick carpet. And every time she did so, she said, "Sit, Margot," in a voice that sounded, rasp and all, remarkably like mine.

At twenty months she recovered from a mild cold very quickly and with little need for the oxygen mask. She had even learned, it turned out, to blow her nose and to cough to clear her throat. We decided that it probably had been by watching Hilary who had repeatedly tried to demonstrate these skills to her sister. It seemed clear that the time for closing her trachea was not far off.

She needed only a little help from me to progress from crawling to cruising to walking. By her second birthday she could get up from the floor in the middle of a room with no help and walk to the nearest chair. And then it was time for her yearly trip to the medical center.

This time she was a quite normal, Terrible-Two patient, utterly uncooperative and assertive. But the specialists were able to establish that her lung capacity had risen from less than 40 percent of normal to well over 50 percent, and her resistance to infection was much greater than it had been. They closed the trachea. She came home with no tube, no rasp, and a sweet little voice in which to pronounce her Terrible-Two "No!"

After that she needed little help from me. She ate ravenously, putting on weight she had good use for and also burning a lot of it with vigorous romps, such as climbing onto the couch, bouncing up and down, jumping off, running around it, then repeating the whole process. From the beginning of this sort of thing her parents wisely refrained from doing anything to inhibit it. She gets breathless fairly soon but, when she does, she just matter-of-factly sits down and waits until she has her breath back.

When she reached three, the county provided a home teacher for her three mornings a week because the pediatrician decided she was still too vulnerable to be in close contact with a lot of other small children and their bugs in a nursery school. But she has her sister and two cousins to play with at home. And by the time she's six it is highly likely she will be able to go to school.

The last time I saw her, Erica showed me a drawing Margot had done. It shows a child under an oxygen tent in a huge bed. And in one upper corner of the tent is a sun with a smiling face.

15
Last Words on New Beginnings

In THE FIRST PAGE I stated that the birth of a baby with great and obvious deformities can shock all concerned but also can lead to transfiguring love. I hope, now that you have read about these children, that I have proved my case. But I also hope I have shown that such transfiguration has to be earned. Unless earned with deep commitment and long, hard effort, it *is* a mere pretense that one can fool oneself with only now and then.

Commitment and hard work are not the whole story, however. The birth of a handicapped baby puts the parents through a long and potentially exhausting emotional ordeal. As demonstrated in some of the case histories I have outlined, not all parents have the strength to take it. But here are some suggestions that I think may help those who need to develop the necessary stamina.

Most parents of children with disabilities go through several stages in their reactions to the discovery of what fate has done to them:

First, almost inevitably, grief.

Second, guilt, which may be so overwhelming that it quickly overtakes and blots out the grief.

Third, denial, refusal to accept the facts.

Fourth, anger, a natural sequel when denial fails.

Fifth, fear and withdrawal.

Sixth, coping and realistic hope.

There is nothing original about this list. Several others who have written about the problems of parents of handicapped children have offered similar outlines of emotional

196

reactions. But some of the parents I have worked with have taken such outlines much too seriously.

"You see," one mother told me, "I have worked through my anger stage, but instead of going on to fear, I've slipped back into guilt."

The first time I encountered such a misunderstanding, it seemed funny. But meeting other such parents again and again taught me better. Those who misunderstand in this way are desperate for help, for guidance, and it is only natural that they take too literally any advice that seems good.

I make this point in the hope that it will help to free readers from any feeling of compulsion. The reactions described do sometimes occur exactly in the order given but more often they do not. Sometimes the first reaction is anger, sometimes denial, sometimes guilt. Some parents shift back and forth repeatedly over the whole range. My purpose is not to prescribe how to react but to describe how other parents have reacted in the hope that awareness of sharing will make the suffering more bearable.

GRIEF

It is not merely unavoidable. One should not even *want* to avoid it. When I first learned that my twenty-month-old daughter had been born with dislocated hips and that it might be too late to repair them properly, my grief was sudden, drastic, and, I felt, an end to the pleasant life I had been living.

One mother I worked with expressed it vividly: "All my usual feelings seemed to evaporate. They changed into a cloud of sadness. It blotted out everything."

It is this intensity of grief that provides the justification that may be felt to be necessary for those professionals who try to stay aloof in order to avoid "burnout." Some pediatricians, for instance, are likely to tell the parents of a badly and unexpectedly handicapped baby exactly what the trouble is in tones as dry and technical as possible, then refer them to specialists, and bow out. I have known parents who, after telling me that they had been treated this way, have gone on to say they thought it was the best way.

But I have never heard any parents complain of their physicians being *too* emotional, *too* sympathetic. One mother told me that she felt the reason she had been able to stay sane after learning that her baby had been born with missing limbs was that the pediatrician who told her sat down beside her, held her hand, and cried with her. And one doctor I know well told me: "I can handle it pretty well while I'm discussing procedures, referrals, and answering questions about handicaps that are going to be lifelong. But after I leave the parents, I have to find a place where I can be by myself and let some tears flow."

Some parents—like Pam, who even while the tears flowed, went right to work doing what she could for Karen—pass through the grief stage in hours or days. Most, however, take at least a few weeks to work through the greater part of it. One mother told me that even after a year she would sometimes find herself crying while doing something routine, such as washing dishes. Another would occasionally wake up in the morning in tears. A third mother would break down and weep unexpectedly whenever she found herself watching a television commercial about baby clothes or food or diapers.

The early birthdays cause some parents to feel renewals of their grief. One year old—two years old—these are great milestones in our society, and with them go awareness that by such a time the baby should be walking, talking, or developing in some other way. When one's child is not developing normally, the milestone can hurt. And so can the birth of a healthy baby to another family member or close friend. One mother of a moderately handicapped two-year-old told me she could not visit the hospital where her brother's first child was born.

"It's where I had my baby. The memory is still too fresh."

Her niece was six weeks old before she could relax and even go to see her at home.

Sometimes meeting other mothers in supermarkets with their children can be hard to take, too. One mother of a severely handicapped sixteen-month-old boy was in tears when she told me of such an encounter.

"I was so pleased that Sonny had finally got the hang of sitting up in the baby seat in the grocery cart. I still had to wedge my purse in one side and an eggplant or something on the other, but he was secure enough to seem to like it and to look around a little as we went up and down the aisles. Well, yesterday we were wheeling along, and here came a woman wheeling her baby, and we met in front of the cake mixes. Her baby was a little bigger than Sonny, and he was knocking things off the shelves, pushing things out of the cart, trying to stand up, and yelling "ma-ma, ma-ma." Sonny was just sitting there, draped over the eggplant. I asked her how old her baby was. She said eight months. I broke down and bawled right there in front of Betty Crocker."

For almost all the parents of handicapped infants I have known, their grief has gradually become more bearable. For some it continues to well up briefly now and then. For others it seems to disappear altogether.

"He just fits into the family so easily," was the way one mother explained to me how she had outdistanced her grief. "He's no problem at all. Anyone could do it."

This last is an exaggeration, of course, but how much of one I do not know. As the stories I have told in this book indicate, however, only a small minority of the families I have worked with have been utterly unable to cope. What's more, most of them have eventually said to me and to their physicians: "If you ever have parents who want to talk, parents of another baby like mine, please call me. I'd like to be able to help anyone going through what I went through."

Those who work through their grief know that they are stronger.

GUILT

Grief is a necessity. Guilt is not. It is a luxury that takes your mind, time, and energy away from things you can and must do that badly need all of your attention they can get.

My saying this, of course, makes little difference to those who feel guilty. What will make *some* difference, I hope, is my assurance that it is a passing phase, a rapidly passing one for most mothers. (In my experience it is almost exclusively a mother's problem. Although a neurotic father doubtless could invent reasons for feeling guilty, I have never known one who did so with much conviction.)

My own flirtation with guilt was a typical mild case. When I found out that my daughter, Laura, then almost twenty months old, had been born with dislocated hips, I had no trouble finding reasons for blaming myself. Few mothers of handicapped infants do. There is always something one did before, during, or after pregnancy at which one can hurl one's own accusations.

The long trip I made by air to Kenya while pregnant and the pills I took against air sickness on that trip were good candidates. But I made inquiries and discovered, as mothers usually do, that there was no known connection between such activities while pregnant and congenital dislocation of the hips. Another excuse for feeling guilty was my profession. Laura's slowness in learning to walk unaided, in contrast with her quickness in other things, should have worried me sooner. And so on.

What made my case of guilt so mild was that I was able to get to work helping Laura soon after discovering that she did have a problem. And that is the prescription for coping with the kind of guilt that stays within hailing distance of reality. Getting down to work, doing what you can to help your child, will leave you little time to moon over what you should or should not have done.

That advice—get to work on the problem—also works

best when the guilt is not just barely within the realm of reality but all too possibly real. Mothers who smoke heavily, drink heavily, or take hard drugs during pregnancy are greatly increasing the chances that they will produce a handicapped baby. But none of those I have worked with has admitted such genuine guilt, so I have no evidence on how well the prescription might work.

More common, in my experience, is persistent unrealistic guilt. Some parents seem to feel a need to be very nearly omnipotent where their children are concerned, to smooth their paths in all directions and keep them always in perfect health. For anyone with a neurotic obsession of this sort, the birth of a handicapped baby is a shattering experience. They sometimes fasten on strange ways of pinpointing their feeling of guilt.

"It was all those potatoes I ate," one mother I worked with told me the first time I saw her.

We talked this over at considerable length, and by the time I left that day I felt I had persuaded her that the potatoes had done her baby no harm. I saw her again a week later.

"It was all those potatoes I ate," she informed me.

In such a case, the best I can do is to suggest that the mother talk with her clergyman or a social worker, psychologist, or other professional counselor. In this particular case a social worker was able to help her spend more of her time working with her baby and less of it blaming herself and those silly potatoes. But for months afterward she would still occasionally mention them.

DENIAL

This sounds like an absolute no-no. It is not, or at least not necessarily. For several mothers I have worked with, it has been very helpful.

"I just couldn't believe it," one of them told me, "when

the pediatrician said that Caroline had Down's syndrome. She looked to me like a perfectly normal new baby. He was saying that she was like the children I had seen in a film shown in my college class in psychology. I just knew it wasn't so.

"It was lucky for me that the lab work took three weeks. When the chromosome count came back confirming the diagnosis, I had moved a little closer to being able to accept it. By then it was obvious that she was very limp. I could still think, when I wanted to, that it was just a muscle problem, but admitting to myself that she had some problem made it easier to begin to consider the rest of what Down's syndrome meant."

I got involved in helping her at about that point, and I remember how slow and tentative she was about every new suggestion I offered. She almost bit my head off when I started to tell her about a book on Down's syndrome babies.

"Everybody's always trying to make me read something," she said, sort of spitting out the words.

A month or so later she asked me about that book. Eventually she became a very competent mother to her daughter, coping as well as anyone could hope to. It took her time to get there, and denial was the way she went about buying herself that time.

In my experience denial works like this far more often than the way it did for Marcia, Duncan's mother, in the story I told earlier about her endless search for a nonexistent "cure." That is the only case I know of in which it went that far. Of course, there are many levels of denial between these two extremes.

The most common, potentially unhealthy kind of denial is a result of changing attitudes about raising a family. Only a generation or so ago most couples who got married did so with the more or less conscious intention of having children, usually right away. Today, certainly many and possibly most couples have doubts about becoming parents, about the drastic change in their way of life that is involved in taking on the twenty-four-hour-a-day task of raising an infant. When the infant presents them with all the extra demands that a handicapped one must, together with the prospect that those demands will continue for many years longer than those of a healthy child, an urge to deny the existence of the handicap is easy to understand.

The best thing I have found to do for parents temporarily stopped at this stage is to introduce them to other families with both handicapped and fully healthy children. A picnic of several such families may be the ideal kind of introduction. On such an occasion the kids are strictly kids, get filthy, eat each other's cookies, take each other's toys, cry a lot, and yell a lot. All of which makes the handicaps look much less fearsome.

ANGER

A physician I know who has worked with many handicapped children insists that all parents of such children must inevitably feel anger. Some, he says, may suppress it but probably would be better off expressing it in some way. The anger may focus on God, the gods, one or more professionals involved in the case, one's spouse, one's parents, one's in-laws. Or just anyone handy.

He may be right, but I don't think so. Many of the parents I have worked with have, indeed, expressed anger, some a great deal of it. However, a considerable number have not, and not all of these, I feel sure, were merely suppressing it.

I know that I, myself, felt none about Laura's dislocated hips, and I had a readily available focus for it if I had felt any. The obstetrician who failed to check for this condition could have been considered at fault. It was a decidedly minor fault, however, and I had no need to suppress any feelings about it. To be sure, the handicap was correctable and corrected within a few months. Had it proved otherwise, I might have felt differently. Some of the parents I have worked with, however, have had to deal with the gravest, lifelong handicaps and have dealt with them with no show of anger and no symptoms of suffering from suppressing it.

I say all this because parents of handicapped children these days are quite likely sooner or later to meet amateur psychoanalysts who will urge them to "let it all hang out," "it," in this case, meaning anger. If you don't happen to feel any, I suggest you tell such advisers to go to hell. That will make them think they have proved their point and enable them to go away happy.

Certainly a little suppression is far better than the kind of total abandonment to anger I have witnessed in a few cases. One father of a child suffering Down's syndrome made himself a nuisance for several months. He would show up at gatherings of parents of handicapped children and dominate the proceedings with tirades against the obstetrician who had delivered his daughter, the pediatrician who had told the parents of her condition, and the medical profession in general. Even if his denunciations had made sense, they would have been unpleasant and out of place.

Of course, physicians do make mistakes. Some are blatant. In such cases they may deserve to hear loud and long objections from their victims, perhaps even to face lawsuits. But it is so difficult for laymen to judge such matters that not once in my experience has the degree of a parent's anger matched the extent of a physician's failure.

One appropriate and effective expression of anger at a health professional I witnessed was occasioned by the all-too-common health biz failing—insensitivity. It happened in a neurosurgeon's office. I was present just to hold the parents' hands. Their daughter suffered the water-on-the-brain problem I have described and had had a shunt placed shortly after birth to solve it. She was now fourteen months old and had been brought to see the doctor because she seemed to be suffering severe head pains.

Surgeon: "The shunt is failing. We'll have to replace it. Don't worry. These things happen."

Father: "Replace it? How?"

Surgeon: "It's a simple procedure." Followed by jargon confusing even to me, and I hear it regularly.

Mother: "You mean an operation?"

Surgeon: "It's a very simple procedure." More jargon.

Father: (Beginning to get stirred up.) "An operation on her head? That's simple?"

Surgeon: "These procedures are routine." More jargon.

Mother: (Really angry now.) "You have to shave her head again, don't you?" She made it sound like an accusation of attempted rape and murder.

With that she at last got through the white gown to the man wearing it. She glared. He gaped. Finally, he looked penitent.

"I'm sorry," he said. "Yes, we will have to shave part of her head. And, yes, it is an operation. She will even be in a very little danger. But there is no alternative." He went on to explain and reexplain in plain English until the parents understood exactly what he was talking about.

I have read arguments to the effect that when parents of handicapped children deliberately refrain from expressing their anger it can provide a sort of fuel from which to obtain some of the energy they need to deal with the problems they keep encountering. This sounds a bit fancy, but there may be something to it. One mother of a child with cerebral palsy wore a chip on her shoulder when she first started taking her son about in public.

"If a stranger even glanced at us, I seethed," she told me. "And if someone actually asked a question about Johnny, I was likely to explode. Until I saw the light.

"I realized that people who asked questions were likely to have children of their own. Answering their questions was like putting money in the bank. Some day their children might be in school with Johnny and be a lot more understanding because I had once taken the time to answer their parents' questions. Now I have a regular speech to make and practically lie in wait for strangers at the supermarket."

That is, indeed, a wonderful way to channel anger and make it work for you.

FEAR AND WITHDRAWAL

For our ancestors mooching about in the wilderness, anger and fear had a lot in common. Sudden danger, a quick spurt of adrenalin, and they were all set for either fight or flight. Which action was chosen depended on the situation and the experience and temperament of the individual.

Nowadays it often is not easy to see the connection. Except in some asphalt jungles, both the urban kind and the highway kind, dangers are usually not so sudden. Many of those we experience are imaginary, slow in becoming apparent to us and long persistent. And worst of all for many people facing modern dangers, there is no place to which they can flee.

Certainly, such is the case for parents of handicapped infants. Those whose temperaments do not permit them an outlet for anger can feel horribly vulnerable. They sometimes try to avoid or cut off as many as possible of their contacts with the outside world. A mother who reacts this way may want to have nothing to do with anyone but her child, her husband, and her physician.

There is nothing necessarily wrong with this way of dealing with the problem in the early stages. To some people that will seem a shocking statement. How can such withdrawal be condoned?

In my experience it can be just another stratagem for gaining time to make necessary changes in one's outlook, plans, and way of life. Some do this by denying that there is anything wrong. Some do it by flaring out angrily at anyone handy. And some can only withdraw into a cocoon of fear.

If the withdrawal persists, it can become a psychiatric problem far beyond the reach of anything I can say here. Preachments about "facing reality" and such would be plain silly, even addressed to those only temporarily withdrawn. No one in that state of mind is going to read a book like this. The only ones involved to whom I can address anything of potential usefulness are the relatives, friends, and neighbors of parents who have withdrawn from them.

In some cases such bystanders do a great deal to cause or reinforce a withdrawal. One mother-in-law I heard of is a prime example.

"You have ruined my son's life," she informed her daughter-in-law when the latter wanted to keep her Down's syndrome baby rather than trying to find an institution or foster parents for it.

Obviously, there is nothing I can say here that would make any difference to an ogress like this. But if you know of a couple with a newborn handicapped baby, do all you can to keep away any family member who might possibly make such a hideous attack on the vulnerable parents.

On the other hand, don't try to be too helpful. Trying to force your attention on a mother who has chosen temporary withdrawal can be as bad as letting her see you shudder and turn away. Give her time. And when it is appropriate to let her know that you care, the old-fashioned covered dish is, in my experience, an excellent opening move. If she is not even answering her doorbell yet, you can leave it on the step with a note letting her know that you sympathize and are available if and when she wants to see you.

When she does, say as little as possible. If you can find something positive to remark on about the baby's appearance or behavior, great. But don't force it. Mostly, just listen. And listen. And listen. It may be as great a service as you ever do for anyone.

COPING AND HOPING

In her book *On Death and Dying*, which first brought to wide public attention the idea that a profound emotional experience can take one through several different stages, Elizabeth Kübler-Ross called the last stage, the goal toward which a dying person should strive, acceptance. Some other writers on the subject of living with handicapped children have recommended the same goal. I don't think it is quite appropriate.

The mother of a year-old boy with cerebral palsy once told me that a friend had congratulated her about the way she had accepted her son's problem.

"I knew she meant well," the mother said to me, "but she sure misunderstood. Accept it is something I'll never do. There isn't a day goes by I don't wish he was normal. I've just learned to cope as well as I can and to keep my hopes realistic."

That, to my mind, is a far better way to describe the goal to strive toward—coping and realistic hoping. In a very few cases the only realistic hope is no hope, but one can always learn to cope. Even when all that can sensibly mean is finding an acceptable institution.

If you happen to be a mother alone with your recently born first baby, and that baby has a handicap that means a lot of extra work for you, my assertion that "one can always learn to cope" may seem lofty and condescending. But, believe me, it's true. I make it, and stand by it, only because I have known many mothers who have learned to cope with the remarkably difficult, round-the-clock problems presented by some kinds of handicaps.

Indeed, if you are a mother home alone with your first baby, learning to cope is not likely to seem a cinch even when the baby is perfectly healthy. You have round-the-clock problems, and there's nothing easy about them until you get the hang of it all. If the baby has a handicap, you need help. The first step in learning to cope is to learn to *ask* for that help. You probably will be surprised at how much of it is available and how enthusiastically it will be provided.

In some areas, some kinds of help may be offered even before you ask. If your baby was born in a hospital, the attending nurses or physicians may have alerted any local government agencies or private organizations concerned with handicapped children, and one of these may send someone to see you before you go home. But this, obviously, is not something you can depend on. Some potentially helpful agencies may be prevented by law from offering help before it is requested, and others may feel that to do so would be intruding on your privacy.

So you probably will have to ask. Start with the physician who delivered your baby or with the pediatrician or other specialist who helped make the diagnosis. If they seem too remote to approach, try one of the nurses. Or ask whether the hospital has someone who can help you find help.

I don't mean to suggest, of course, that you will be reading this book and following these suggestions while you are still in the hospital and right after learning about your baby's handicap. It is far more likely that you will be at home, still trying to get used to the whole situation, and making your inquiries by telephone or letter. In a moment I will get down to specifics about the kinds of help you can ask or look for and the variety of sources from which you can get it. But right here I want to offer an example supporting my point about the surprising amount of help that is available.

A friend of mine is the mother of a three-year-old girl with Down's syndrome. The child, Ilmi, walks well and is pretty independent and self-motivated but is not yet fully potty trained. She speaks only Finnish, the family being new immigrants. Her mother asked me whether there was any hope of finding a nursery school program where Ilmi could spend a few hours or so a day during the summer, and I volunteered to look into it for her.

My starting point was in the Yellow Pages of our local telephone directory. Under "Nursery Schools" I was referred to two other classifications: "Child Care Centers" and "School—Pre-School & Kindergarten (Academic)." Under these I found more than forty entries scattered around our county, which has a population of about 200,000. I narrowed those forty possibilities to eight by choosing only those within a few miles of my friend's home.

Two of the eight could not take Ilmi because they were equipped only for the potty trained. Three others felt that they could cope with her but had no room for another child in their forseeable futures. The director of one of these said he would be delighted to have her if and when a vacancy did develop, that he already had two handicapped children, and that several of the parents of the normal toddlers in his school were highly pleased by the presence of those two. These parents, he said, felt that handicapped classmates helped to widen the horizons of their children.

The three other schools all were willing and able to take Ilmi. All were licensed schools and seemed to have, as far as I could determine, unblemished reputations. We finally chose the one where she could spend the most time—two hours a morning, three days a week.

Doubtless, there are parts of the country where the possibilities would be fewer. There are others where you would find many more.

So, since I entitled this section "Coping and Hoping," what about hoping? My answer is that coping *is* the only kind of hoping that seems to me worth much—the kind of realistic hoping in which you automatically and enthusiastically should want to invest time and effort. To hope for better things for your handicapped baby without putting in a great deal of effort to make the hope come true is to prepare yourself for misery.

SPECIFICS FOR COPING

1. GETTING INFORMATION

You need all the information you can handle. You need information about handicapped babies in general, like that provided in this book, plus information about the specific handicap or handicaps of your child. You need information about the services and advice available in your area and about the educational opportunities that will be available in the future.

As already suggested, the personnel of the hospital where your baby was born, or the professionals involved if it was a home birth, are the natural sources of such information for you to start with. They should be able to refer you to other local sources of information and help. And they may be able to give you the names and addresses of county, state, and national organizations and publications from which you can get more. In addition, the appendix of this book lists organizations and publications to which you can write for specific kinds of information.

2. SPREADING INFORMATION

As soon as you can do so, start telling your family and friends about your baby's problems. If you have to go through a phase of denying that there's a problem or of withdrawing from the whole thing, you have to. But you will find that the sooner you start talking about it the easier the talking will be for all concerned.

If you have older children, try to talk to them, too, in the simplest language possible. You may be surprised at how understanding they can be.

Once, when I arrived for my first visit at the home of a two-month-old with spina bifida and just home from the hospital, the door was opened by her four-year-old sister.

"Amy has a problem," she informed me.

She watched with close attention while I worked with Amy and not once did she try to divert attention to herself. On all my subsequent visits she behaved with similar restraint. When she was out of the room once, I complimented her mother about this, and she attributed it to her frequently discussing Amy's difficulties with the older child.

3. FIND A PHYSICIAN YOU CAN WORK WITH

If you already have a family doctor or pediatrician who will listen to your questions and answer them so that you can understand, count yourself lucky. Skill in communicating is no more common among physicians than among the rest of us.

Some are not only hopeless at it but refuse even to try. This sort seem to persuade themselves that the human beings they treat are just unusually complicated machines. When such a machine asks questions, they pay little or no attention. If you are stuck with such a doctor, you have to look for a better one.

On the other hand, don't expect saintliness. Not all your questions will be answerable. Also, asking the same ones over and over is guaranteed to wear out anyone's patience. And a physician who is good at explaining things is likely to have a lot of patients in need of her or his time.

Keep looking until you find a sympathetic physician, and then learn to be reasonable in your demands.

4. BABY FIRST, HANDICAP SECOND

When I discovered that my daughter, Laura, had congenitally dislocated hips, she was almost two years old, the age of assertiveness, and she was naturally self-assertive to start with. She never gave me a chance to ignore her as a person and concentrate my attention on her hip problem. Later, when I started working with the families of handicapped children, I discovered that we had been lucky that Laura was such a handful. Handicaps can be so overwhelming that they completely distort not only the mother and child relationship but the family's whole life.

It is impossible to list all the ways in which concentrating on the baby rather than on the handicap can make a big difference. Handicaps do not scream, vomit, mess their diapers, have ear infections and chickenpox, fall off couches. Babies do these things. All babies. To make the handicap responsible is to torment yourself endlessly and pointlessly.

The wide ramifications of this can be described in terms of babysitting. Some of the families I have worked with at first considered it downright immoral even to think of trying to find a babysitter. In a very few cases it is true that a sitter may need a little special training to deal with the baby's problem, but this is unusual. In no case is it doing your baby any good to wear yourself to a frazzle by refusing all chance of respite.

If there is realistic reason to doubt that the usual teenager can cope for a couple of hours, look for a nurse's aide or a practical nurse. Or, better still, train someone yourself—perhaps some relative, friend, or neighbor. Many of these will offer help, and some will actually come through for you.

When Laura was in her body cast, and my son, Chris, in a nursery school, I had a trade-a-kid arrangement with a neighbor. It gave me one wonderful day a week all to myself. The neighbor had three highly mobile hellions for me to "sit" (seldom has the term been less apt) in return, but I never had the slightest doubt about the bargain being worthwhile.

Having someone else to depend on for a few hours actually is a very good step in the right direction for your child, too. Overprotectiveness is an almost inevitable tendency among the parents of handicapped babies. Choosing a sitter is a good first step toward curbing this tendency.

Occasionally, you may have babysitting or similar help almost thrust on you. I have known families that were actually alarmed by such offers because they felt that to accept them would be to become obligated to repayments and they saw no way to repay those offering the help. My feeling is that it is better to pass such kindness on later to someone else who needs it the way you do now. It is a great way to increase the total amount of helpfulness in the world.

One example of the kind of thing I have in mind involves a family I know that has a two-year-old with cerebral palsy. A ten-year-old girl who lives in the neighborhood knocked on the door one afternoon and asked if she could play with the baby.

"At first," the mother of the two-year-old told me, "I was very skeptical, of course, but she is absolutely wonderful with the baby. She comes almost every afternoon for an hour or two. And the great result is that I get to fix dinner without a screamer wrapped around my ankles."

More common are volunteers to drive your older children to school on rainy days or to get you tickets to a concert or to help mow your lawn. To be negative about such offers seems to me a sad and misguided way of refusing to let the world become a slightly better place.

5. PARENTS' GROUPS

Probably in all cities and in most towns and suburban areas of any size you will find organizations, mostly informal, of parents of handicapped children. None that I know of assesses dues or imposes any other obligations. Their basic purpose is mutual support, advice, and occasionally a little practical assistance. Anyone in your area who is involved with handicapped children should be able to help you find such a group. I strongly advise attending at least a meeting or two to see if it's for you.

The group in my area is mostly social and goes in for potluck dinners and the handing down of toys, clothes, and equipment that have been outgrown. Now and then a pediatrician, psychologist, teacher, nurse, or therapist will be asked to give an informal talk and answer questions. But I have heard of other, more ambitious groups that go in for training babysitters for the severely handicapped and pooling their services.

One such group arranged to be notified by the local hospital whenever the parents of a handicapped newborn needed help that they could provide. Among those referred to them were the young and terrified parents of a Down's syndrome baby. The parents of a four-year-old Down's syndrome child volunteered to take the newborn home with them until the young couple could pull themselves together. That took only a week, and the two families have become very close, to the benefit not only of both families but also of the total supply of good will and harmony in the world at large.

6. TOUGHEN YOURSELF TO TACTLESSNESS

As I mentioned earlier, there have been times in the world's history when a person with a noticeable handicap was considered to be out of favor with God and therefore a proper subject for torment. Not everyone alive today has progressed beyond that hideous stage. Also, if your child looks strikingly different from ordinary, an occasional stranger may be startled into a reaction he or she will quickly regret.

Advice like "Don't let them bother you" is not only of little use but probably bad. I would rather say—let them bother you, if they do. By which I mean, don't try to kid yourself that such things don't hurt. For some people a flash of anger is the best way to react. For others, telling family and friends about such incidents can help. In my experience anything is better than trying to ignore or forget them.

Other cruelties are built into the situation. If your three-year-old is unable to walk well and is out on a lawn with two-year-olds who are zooming about in the usual two-year-old way, the sight hurts. So do the shrill, jeering "What's the matter with you?" kind of questions other children are bound to address to yours, not to mention the occasional attempts at striking, throwing things, spitting, and such. About this I can only remind you that in our society it is an extremely rare and not necessarily fortunate child who does not both suffer and perpetrate at least a few small cruelties in the course of learning to live with other children.

7. TOYS AND EQUIPMENT

Whether or not their children have handicaps, some parents feel that by showering them with toys they can "make up for things." If the child has a handicap, what's being made up for seems obvious. In my experience it often is quite hidden. In such cases what's being atoned for is the parents' feeling of guilt about not giving the child all the time, thought, concern, love they feel should be provided.

That guilt may or may not be realistic. I suspect that as often as not the parents who feel it are making excessive demands on themselves on behalf of their children. But the worst of it is that children can learn to look on and demand toys as expressions of parental concern and love—of which, of course, they can never have more than enough.

My own feeling is that toys, and especially those for handicapped children, should be few, simple, and safe. Often, the best ones are homemade or improvised. Were it not for advertising, I doubt that any child would prefer one of those hideously "realistic" and complicated store-bought dolls, destined to quick breakage, over a rag doll sewn by the mother or grandmother. And kitchen implements without sharp edges or other sources of danger make fascinating playthings for most children.

As for the kind of equipment some handicapped children need, such as braces, walkers, and wheelchairs, the charges are often among the most disgraceful gouging in health biz today. They are worse even than hospital charges. Not once but several times I have known makers of braces to spend three or four hours turning twenty or thirty dollars worth of raw materials into something for which they charge five hundred dollars or more. Even insurance companies, which do little or nothing to resist hospital gouging, are attempting to set limits on how much they will spend on equipment for the handicapped.

So, if you need such equipment, do everything you can to avoid having to buy it new. Look all over the place to try to find something you can borrow or rent. And if you have to buy something new and are covered by insurance, make sure everything works before you accept delivery. The fine print may let the company off from paying for any adjustments or replacements.

Or, best of all, try to find someone in your family or among your friends who can make it for you. One father I know wanted parallel bars for his partially paralyzed son to hold onto while learning to walk. New, the best approximation to what he wanted would have cost several hundred dollars. He made what he wanted out of ten dollars worth of plastic pipe and some boards he found lying around his back yard.

Another family wanted a wheelchair with a few special features. Among other things, they wanted the height adjustable so that it could be made low enough to fit under the dining room table and high enough to fit at the kitchen counter so that the child could watch her mother work. Shopping among the equipment makers, they concluded that the cheapest possibility would come to more than a thousand dollars. A friend heard about this and helped them make a cardboard model of what they needed. They took the model to a local carpenter. Out of plywood padded with foam rubber and covered with Naugahyde, he made exactly what they wanted. He charged them one hundred and fifty dollars.

THE FUTURE

Today in this country things are better for the handicapped than they ever have been before. The heart of the improvement, I think, is the tremendous increase in the public's awareness not only that handicapped people exist in large numbers but also that they have, in addition to their extraordinariness, quite ordinary interests and needs. Both cause and effect of this improvement is the trend known in public schools as mainstreaming—teaching handicapped children in classrooms with ordinary children their age whenever this can be done without too great a burden on teachers or too great expense in modifying facilities. The improvement is caused by bringing the handicapped into more frequent contact with the rest of us. The effect of the improvement is that the first steps in this direction have made the following ones much easier and more popular.

One of the motives for mainstreaming, of course, is to save money for school districts and taxpayers, but this is not necessarily mere crass materialism. Special classes for the handicapped can be extremely and wastefully expensive. To be sure, if saving money becomes the chief motive for mainstreaming, the result may be very hard on some children because mainstreaming simply does not work for all of them. In its general effect, however, I think mainstreaming has been very much for the good, no matter what the principal motivation.

My favorite example of mainstreaming at its best from the child's point of view is the case of Miranda. She was a victim of cerebral palsy, and I worked with her at home for two years. At the age of three she was ready for preschool but definitely not for an ordinary or mainstream preschool. She could walk, but only slowly and with the aid of a walker. She could talk, but also only slowly and with some words unintelligible. And she drooled quite a bit. No ordinary preschool could have provided all the help she needed.

Instead of entering a preschool for normal children, she attended a class for physically handicapped children for four years. Every day she worked for an hour or so one-on-one with a physical therapist and the same with a speech therapist. By the end of those four years she not only walked without the walker but could even break into an only slightly awkward run. Her words were completely intelligible. And the drooling was a rare occurrence.

Her parents also worked with her during those years, of course, and very imaginatively. Typically, when they found that the ordinary kinds of pets all moved too fast for her, they got her a turtle. Pushing it around in the pram specially made for it, she was the envy of the neighborhood kids.

And so at the age of seven Miranda was the ideal candidate for mainstreaming. When she entered the second grade of the nearest elementary school, she was different from the other kids, and no mistaking. She read at the fourth-grade level. She wrote stories and poems of her own on a typewriter. And she had the well-earned self-confidence of an Olympic medalist.

Although Miranda's cerebral palsy is still noticeable in her awkward walk and other movements, these difficulties do not mean that she needs any extra attention from her teacher. That is what makes her mainstreaming a total and unquestioned success. A teacher already over-burdened with thirty-odd ordinary children in a class simply does not have the time that many of the physically handicapped must be given.

Fortunately, there are ways out of this difficulty. If a child needs extra attention, not while sitting at a desk, going to the toilet, and performing other regular functions, but in the form of extra physical or speech therapy or such, these can be provided after school. If full mainstreaming is out of the question, it can be experienced partially in the form of shared recesses, music, art, or such. In some schools teacher's aides provide some small extra attentions needed by the mildly handicapped.

In my area we have found that the local university's school of education is a good source of such aides. Students of child development often need field work or research projects.

Working as volunteer aides, they can be just what is needed to help mainstream the handicapped.

Recently, a social worker at the local health agency with which I work approached the director of the university laboratory school for toddlers. Its only previous experience with handicapped children had been with a girl who wore a hearing aid, but the director was intrigued by the idea of trying others. Now two three-year-olds, one with Down's syndrome and one with a muscle disorder, are attending two mornings a week.

Such developments plus seemingly minor but actually basic other ones, like access to public buildings via ramps and dropped curbs so that those in wheelchairs can cross streets unaided, are what have made possible a pleasant little scene I witnessed not long ago. It was at the checkout counter of my neighborhood supermarket. A young woman with cerebral palsy was paying for her purchase and having a little trouble fishing change from her wallet. Neither the clerk nor anyone in the line showed any impatience. And when the transaction was at last completed, the clerk said, "Have a nice day, Joanne."

This level of acceptance and ease bodes well for the future of the handicapped.

APPENDIX A

Reading List for Children

THERE ARE a number of pertinent books written especially for children. Check with your local children's librarian. I have read all these listed below and can recommend them.

ARTIFICIAL LIMBS

About Handicaps
An open family book for parents and children together
Sara Bonnett Stein
Walker & Company, New York, 1974

Excellent presentation of physical handicaps. Deals specifically with artificial limbs and cerebral palsy. 6–10 years

Don't Feel Sorry for Paul
Bernard Wolf
J.B. Lippincott, Philadelphia & New York, 1974

Two weeks in the life of a seven-year-old boy who wears three artificial limbs. Good photographs. 6–10 years

BLINDNESS/VISUAL IMPAIRMENT

A Cane in Her Hand
Ada B. Litchfield
Albert Whitman & Company, Chicago, 1977

The frustrations and accomplishments of a visually handicapped girl. 6–10 years.

Connie's New Eyes
Bernard Wolf
J.B. Lippincott, Philadelphia & New York, 1976

Beautiful photographs and sensitive story of how a Seeing Eye dog is raised and trained. Follows the life of a young woman teacher who is blind. 8 years and older

CEREBRAL PALSY

Tracy
Nancy Mack
Raintree Editions,
Milwaukee, WI, 1976

Follows the everyday life of
a young girl with cerebral
palsy integrated into regular
school. Good photographs.
6–10 years

About Handicaps
An open family book for
parents and children together
Sara Bonnett Stein
Walker & Company, New
York, 1974

Excellent presentation of
physical handicaps. Deals
specifically with artificial
limbs and cerebral palsy.
6–10 years

DEAFNESS/HEARING LOSS

A Button in Her Ear
Ada B. Litchfield
Albert Whitman &
Company, Chicago, 1976

A little girl with a hearing
loss gets a hearing aid.
5–10 years

*I Have a Sister/My Sister
Is Deaf*
Jeanne Whitehouse Peterson
Harper & Row Publishers,
New York, 1977

Describes beautifully what
her sister can and cannot do.
5–10 years

Anna's Silent World
Bernard Wolf
J.B. Lippincott, Philadelphia
& New York, 1977

A six-year-old girl with a
profound hearing loss.
Photographs and text
describe her active life.
6–10 years

DISABILITY

What If You Couldn't
A book about special needs
Janet Kamien
Charles Scribner's Sons,
New York, 1979

Good information about
causes and consequences of
specific handicaps.

LEARNING DISABILITY

Kelly's Creek
Doris Buchanan Smith
Thomas Y. Crowell, New
York, 1975

A nine-year-old boy with a
learning disability learns to
live with his handicap and
build his self-esteem.   8–12
years

RETARDATION

One Little Girl
Joan Fassler
Behavioral Publications,
Inc., New York, 1969

About a slightly retarded
girl who knows she can do
some things quite well.
5–10 years

Between Friends
Sheila Garrigue
Bradbury Press, Scarsdale,
New York, 1978

A sensitive description of a
friendship between a
twelve-year-old and an older
girl with Down's syndrome.
9–13 years

APPENDIX B

Reading List for Parents

THERE ARE a number of books on children and disabilities. I have included those I consider the most helpful in practical ways and the most revealing in inspiring ways.

CHILD DEVELOPMENT

Infants and Mothers
T. Berry Brazleton
Dell Publishing Company,
New York, 1969
Development month by month following a quiet, moderately active, and active baby. Emphasizes the range of normal behavior.

Toddlers and Parents
A Declaration of Independence
T. Berry Brazleton
Delacorte Press, New York, 1974
Emphasizes emotional/psychological development.

The First Twelve Months of Life
Your baby's growth month by month
Frank Caplan, Editor
Grossett & Dunlap, New York, 1973
Growth charts detailing the motor, language, mental, and social developments during each month. Describes in detail the behaviors that are being refined and those that are emerging.

The Second Twelve Months of Life
A kaleidoscope of growth
Frank and Theresa Caplan
Bantam Books, New York, 1981
Describes how new achievements lead to independence and self-help.

How to Parent
Dr. Fitzhugh Dodson
Signet Books, The New
American Library, New
York, 1970

On parenting from birth to
five years, covering physical
and emotional development,
discipline, intellectual
stimulation. Excellent
sections on toys, books,
records, and a reading list
for parents.

Between Parent and Child
Haim Ginott
Avon Books, New York,
1969

Excellent guidance on
discipline. Stresses good
communication of positive
and negative feelings.

The Baby Exercise Book
For the first fifteen months
Dr. Janine Levy
Pantheon Books, New York,
1973

Basic movements and
exercises for babies with
normal or low muscle tone.

You and Your Toddler
Sharing the Developing Years
Dr. Janine Levy
Pantheon Books, New York,
1981

Description of how parents
can encourage, enjoy, and
understand development
from one to three years.

Learningames
For the First Three Years
Joseph Sparling and
Isabelle Lewis
Berkley Books, New York
1981

100 ideas and activities for
any child who is
developmentally 36 months
or younger.

The First Three Years of Life
Burton L. White
Avon Books, New York,
1975

A warm, informative book
detailing physical,
emotional, and intellectual
growth. Includes excellent
suggestions for additional
reading, toys, equipment.

Physically Handicapped Children

A Medical Atlas for Teachers
Eugene E. Bleck, M.D. and
Donal Nagel, M.D., Editors
Grune & Stratton, Harcourt
Brace Jovanovich,
Publishers, New York, 1982

Thoroughly describes
disabling conditions in easily
understood language.
Includes many suggestions
for adaptive aids and
equipment, extensive
reading list, resources for
recreation. (Check to see if
your school district, health
department, or county
medical library has it and
borrow it.)

Helping Your Exceptional Baby

Cliff Cunningham and
Patricia Sloper
Pantheon Books, New York,
1980

A practical program of
games and exercises for
parents to help their child.

A Difference in the Family

Living with a Disabled Child
Helen Featherstone
Basic Books, New York,
1980

Sensitively describes coping,
adjustments, and
accommodations for
incorporating a disabled
child into one's family.

The Chronically Ill Child

A Guide for Parents and
Professionals
Audrey T. McCollum, M.S.
Yale University Press, New
Haven, Conn., 1981

Describes experiences of
many parents and ways that
professionals can give
significant help. Strong
chapters on sources of help,
emotional responses to
diagnosis, and family
relationships.

Raising the Handicapped Child

Laura Pearlman & Kathleen
Anton Scott
Prentice-Hall, Inc.
Englewood Cliffs, New
Jersey, 1981

Shares the common concern
of parents with factual
information on education,
financial aid, medical
treatment, and planning.

Caring for Your Disabled Child
Benjamin Spock, M.D.
Marion O. Lerrigo, Ph.D.
Collier Books, New York, 1965

Discusses parents' roles in finding medical care, rehabilitation, and education, as well as living with disability.

Our Special Child
A Guide to Successful Parenting of Handicapped Children
Bette M. Ross
Walker and Company, New York, 1981

Emphasizes the need for stimulation and play with many practical suggestions. Follows child with Down's syndrome from birth to young adulthood.

Listen to Your Heart
A Message to Parents of Handicapped Children
Elise H. Wentworth
Houghton Mifflin Co., Boston, Mass., 1974

Describes the universal experiences and emotional responses as only the parent of a handicapped child can.

The Exceptional Parent
(magazine)
Psy-Ed Corp.
264 Beacon St., Boston, Mass. 02116

Information and sharing of experiences by and for parents of exceptional children.

Sharing Our Caring
(magazine)
P.O. Box 400
Milton, Washington 98354
Published by parents and professionals interested in the health and welfare of children with Down's syndrome.

The following books go far beyond their stated subject matter. I recommend them to anyone interested in the far reaches of human experience and growth.

AUTISM

A Child Called Noah
A Family Journal
Josh Greenfeld
Holt, Rinehart and Winston, New York, 1972

The early life experiences of an autistic child and his family. Told in journal form with honesty and courage.

Son-Rise
Barry Kaufman
Harper and Row, New York, 1976
Detailed account of efforts made to reach an unreachable child.

The Siege
The First Eight Years of an Autistic Child
Clara Claiborne Park
Harcourt Brace Jovanovich, Inc., New York, 1967
A descriptive and compassionate account of how far love and knowledge can go to reach a child.

APHASIA

A Different Drummer
Constance Carpenter Cameron
Prentice-Hall, Inc., Englewood Cliffs, New Jersey, 1973
A strong story of parental resolution, determination, and hope and the search for help.

CEREBRAL PALSY

Handling the Young Cerebral Palsied Child at Home
Nancie Finnie, F.C.S.P.
E.P. Dutton, New York, 1975
Very readable with clear drawings. Detailed and comprehensive. Highly practical book for anyone involved with children with cerebral palsy or abnormal muscle tone. Includes lists of books, helping agencies, resources for equipment and accessories, toys.

DOWN'S SYNDROME

Growing and Learning
Siegfried M. Pueschel, M.D., Editor
Sheed Andrews and McMeel, Inc., Kansas City, Mo., 1978
Strong sections on early developmental stimulation, feeding, and expectations.

HEMOPHILIA

Journey
Robert and Suzanne Massie
Warner Books, New York, 1976
Powerful account of a family which goes far beyond coping with hemophilia.

HIGH RISK

A Time To Be Born
David Bell, M.D.
William Morrow and Co.,
Inc., New York, 1975
Sensitive and
compassionate. Concerned
with the conflicting issues
and emotions in an intensive
care nursery.

The High Risk Child
A Guide for Concerned Parents
Philip Deppe and
Judith Sherman
Macmillan, New York, 1981
Strong chapters on finding
the right educational
programs.

LEARNING/BEHAVIOR PROBLEMS

P.S. Your Not Listening
Eleanor Craig
Signet, New American
Library, New York, 1972
A teacher describes her own
growth as she works with
severely disturbed children
in a public school.

One Child
Torey Hayden
G.P. Putnam's Sons,
New York, 1980
The intimate account of the
relationship between an
emotionally disturbed child
and her teacher.

Somebody Else's Kids
Torey Hayden
G.P. Putnam's Sons, New
York, 1981
A year in the lives of four
students in a special
education class described by
their sensitive, innovative
teacher.

A Circle of Children
Mary McCracken
J.B. Lippincott, New York,
1973
A teacher who cares about
children and fosters growth
and change.

RETARDATION

Before and After Zachariah
Fern Kupfer
Delacorte Press, New York,
1982
A gripping, realistic look at
how the birth of a severely
handicapped child affects
the life of his family.
Excellent presentation of
alternatives to keeping him
at home.

APPENDIX C

Sources of Information, Advice, and Assistance

Alexander Graham Bell Association for the Deaf Headquarters
3417 Volta Place, N.W.
Washington, D.C. 20007

Answers questions concerning educational programs, general resources. Information brochures on early detection, mainstreaming. Lending library. Also gives scholarships to profoundly deaf college students.

American Council of the Blind
1211 Connecticut Ave., N.W. Suite 506
Washington, D.C. 20036

Information and referral on all aspects of blindness.

American Council of the Blind Parents
Route A, Box 78
Franklin, Louisiana 70438

Affiliated with American Council of the Blind. Focus is parenting (whether the parent and/or child has a visual problem). Newsletter. Can refer individuals to other people in similar situations.

American Foundation for the Blind
15 West 16th Street
New York, N.Y. 10011

Provides direct service including information and referrals, special consumer products including games, extensive publications including magazines in large print.

American Printing House for the Blind, Inc.
P.O. Box 6085
Louisville, Kentucky 40206-0085

Provides textbooks and educational aids for all students of less than college grade, books in Braille and large print.

Association for Retarded Citizens
National Headquarters
2501 Avenue J
Arlington, Texas 76011

Provides free materials to parents. Limited referral and consultation on specific problems. Referral to local ARC unit for support and assistance. Publications.

Clearing House on the Handicapped
Office of Special Education & Rehabilitative Services
Room 3106 Switzer Building
330 C Street, S.W.
Washington, D.C. 20202

Responds to inquiries concerning handicapping conditions and related services. Refers to resources close to inquirer's home.

Closer Look
The National Information Center for the Handicapped
1201 16th Street
Washington, D.C. 20036

National Information and Referral Center providing direction and guidance. Newsletter. Sponsors training seminars for parents.

Crippled Children's Services
For information and address in your state contact:
Director, Maternal & Child Health Service,
Health Services and Mental Health Administration
5600 Fishers Lane
Rockville, Maryland 20852

Provides services to children with orthopedic problems and chromosomal conditions affecting muscles, joints, and bones. May assume all or part of cost of treatment.

Council for Exceptional Children
1920 Association Drive
Reston, Virginia 22091

Supports research and training to improve education of handicapped children. Conducts training. Produces publications.

Epilepsy Foundation of America
4351 Garden City Drive, Suite 406
Landover, Maryland 20785

Information and referral service, including advocacy, support of research, low-cost drugs, and group insurance.

International Association of Parents of the Deaf Inc.
814 Thayer Avenue
Silver Spring, Maryland 20910

Provides information and direct contact to parents of deaf children, sponsors regional convention.

The John Tracy Clinic
806 West Adams Blvd.
Los Angeles, CA. 90007

Offers two courses to parents of deaf children: one covers birth to 2 years; the other from 2 to 6 years. Both are available in English and Spanish. A third course, also available in English and Spanish, is for parents of children with vision and hearing handicaps, no age limit. Parents should request a course in writing and should give the child's name and age and their complete address.

Let's Play To Grow
Joseph P. Kennedy, Jr. Foundation
1701 K. St., N.W. Suite 205
Washington, D.C. 20006

Provides training in teaching and playskills for children with special needs and their families. Provides low-cost materials and play guides in English and Spanish.

Muscular Dystrophy Association
810 Seventh Ave.
New York, N.Y. 10019

Provides medical services to individuals diagnosed with any of 40 neuromuscular diseases. Publishes pamphlets addressing the needs and concerns of parents who have children with neuromuscular diseases.

National Association of the Deaf
814 Thayer Avenue
Silver Spring, Maryland 20910

Information about deafness and related subjects. No direct client services but able to make referrals.

National Association for Visually Handicapped
3201 Balboa Street
San Francisco, Ca. 94121

Produces and distributes large print books, maintains a loan library.
(Those living west of Chicago use the above address)

(Those living east of Chicago use this address)

National Association for Visually Handicapped
22 West 21st Street, 6th floor
New York, N.Y. 10010

Produces and distributes large print books, maintains a loan library.

National Easter Seal Society for Crippled Children and Adults
2023 West Ogden Avenue
Chicago, Illinois 60612

Services are delivered through more than 800 state and local affiliates across the country. Services include: physical, occupational, and speech therapy, transportation, referral and follow-up.

National Genetics Foundation
555 West 57th Street
New York, N.Y. 10019

Can refer to the center most appropriate for diagnosis on treatment of a specific genetic problem, information on genetic counseling, and implications of genetic diseases.

The National Society For Children and Adults With Autism
1234 Massachusetts Avenue, N.W., Suite 1017
Washington, D.C. 20005

An information and referral service providing information on: appropriate evaluation and diagnosis, education and treatment programs and techniques, books and films.

Spina Bifida Association of America
343 South Dearborn St.
Chicago, Illinois 60604

Supplies educational materials, pamphlets, national newsletter, publications; refers parents to local chapters for support and direction.

United Cerebral Palsy Association, Inc.
66 East 34th Street
New York, N.Y. 10016

This is a federation of more than 250 state and local affiliates providing services such as therapy, diagnosis, treatment, infant development programs, preschool education.